Marx: A Very Short Introduction

VERY SHORT INTRODUCTIONS are for anyone wanting a stimulating and accessible way into a new subject. They are written by experts, and have been translated into more than 45 different languages.

The series began in 1995, and now covers a wide variety of topics in every discipline. The VSI library currently contains over 550 volumes—a Very Short Introduction to everything from Psychology and Philosophy of Science to American History and Relativity—and continues to grow in every subject area.

Very Short Introductions available now:

Available soon:

For more information visit our website

www.oup.com/vsi/

Peter Singer

MARX

A Very Short Introduction
SECOND EDITION

OXFORD
UNIVERSITY PRESS

OXFORD
UNIVERSITY PRESS

Great Clarendon Street, Oxford, OX2 6DP,
United Kingdom

Oxford University Press is a department of the University of Oxford.
It furthers the University's objective of excellence in research, scholarship,
and education by publishing worldwide. Oxford is a registered trade mark of
Oxford University Press in the UK and in certain other countries

First published 1980 as an Oxford University Press paperback
Reissued 1996
First published as a Very Short Introduction 2000
Second edition published 2018

Published in the United States of America by Oxford University Press
198 Madison Avenue, New York, NY 10016, United States of America

British Library Cataloguing in Publication Data
Data available

Library of Congress Control Number: 2017962195

ISBN 978-0-19-882107-6

Printed and bound by
CPI Group (UK) Ltd, Croydon, CR0 4YY

Contents

Marx

Preface

The 200th anniversary of Karl Marx's birth is an occasion for a reassessment of his place in history. Was he a 19th-century thinker whose ideas became immensely influential in the 20th century, but have now been discredited? Or did Marx, like Darwin or Einstein, advance our understanding of reality by discovering a truth that still holds today? Perhaps a proper assessment of his significance lies somewhere between those extremes? One of the aims of this book is to answer these questions. My other aim, which is in any case a prerequisite for establishing Marx's significance, is to set out, briefly and clearly, his central ideas. There is now such an abundant literature on Marx that one should think twice before adding another book, even a very slim one, to the stack. I wrote this book because there is a unifying vision that underlies Marx's voluminous work, and I did not know of any other work that presented it in a manner comprehensible to general readers with little or no previous knowledge of Marx's writings. The success of the book's original edition suggests that it did fill a gap in the literature. More recent scholarly work on Marx's ideas has added some additional details and insights. This new edition therefore incorporates this more recent scholarship while giving additional space to evaluating the relevance of Marx's ideas today.

Peter Singer

*Princeton University and
the University of Melbourne*

Acknowledgements

For biographical details of Marx's life, I am indebted to David McLellan's *Karl Marx: His Life and Thought: A Biography*, 4th edition (New York: Palgrave Macmillan, 2006), and Gareth Stedman Jones, *Karl Marx: Greatness and Illusion* (Cambridge, Mass.: Harvard University Press, 2016). For the first edition of this book, I received helpful comments from G. A. Cohen, Robert Heilbroner, Renata Singer, and Marilyn Weltz. The second edition benefited from comments from Charles Bresler, Iason Gabriel, and, especially, Karsten Struhl. Jonathon Catlin assisted me in updating the sources and translations of quotations used in the earlier editions, and made many valuable suggestions that have improved the text. Zusong Lu and Yaqi Liu helped me to understand the significance of Marxism in China today. Justin Maiman told me how many Marxists it takes to change a lightbulb.

The first edition was written in response to an invitation from Keith Thomas and Oxford University Press's Henry Hardy. This edition was suggested by Andrea Keegan, in her capacity as editor responsible for the Very Short Introductions series. I thank her for stimulating me to think again about Marx in the 21st century and I also thank Jenny Nugee of Oxford University Press and Elakkia Bharathi of SPi Global for overseeing the book's production.

List of illustrations

Abbreviations

References in the text to Marx's writings are generally given by an abbreviation of the title, followed by a page reference. Unless otherwise indicated below, these page references are to David McLellan (ed.), *Karl Marx: Selected Writings*, 2nd edition (Oxford: Oxford University Press, 2000).

B	'On Bakunin's *Statism and Anarchy*'
C I	*Capital: A Critique of Political Economy*, volume I, trans. Ben Fowkes (London: Penguin, 1990)
C III	*Capital: A Critique of Political Economy*, volume III, trans. David Fernbach (London: Penguin, 1993)
CM	*Communist Manifesto*
D	Doctoral Thesis
EB	*The Eighteenth Brumaire of Louis Bonaparte*
EPM	*Economic and Philosophical Manuscripts of 1844*
G	*Grundrisse: Foundations of the Critique of Political Economy*, trans. Martin Nicolaus (London: Penguin, 1993)
GI	*The German Ideology*
GP	'Critique of the Gotha Programme'
HF	*The Holy Family*
I	'Towards a Critique of Hegel's *Philosophy of Right*: Introduction'
J	'On the Jewish Question'
M	'On James Mill' (notebook)

Marx

Chapter 1
A life and its legacy

Marx's impact

Marx's influence can be compared to that of major religious figures like Jesus or Muhammad. For much of the second half of the 20th century, nearly four out of every ten people on earth lived under governments that considered themselves Marxist and claimed to follow his ideas in deciding what policies they should implement. In these countries Marx was almost a secular deity. His image was everywhere reverently displayed and his words were considered the ultimate source of truth and authority. Political leaders and their opponents sought to interpret them in ways that suited their political leanings, and the fate of those who lost was similar to that of heretics. The lives of hundreds of millions of people were transformed, for better or for worse, by Marx's legacy.

This influence has not been limited to communist societies. Conservative, liberal, and democratic socialist governments have established social welfare systems to cut the ground from under revolutionary Marxist opposition movements. Other opponents of Marxism have reacted in less benign ways: Mussolini and Hitler were aided in their rise to power by conservative forces that saw them as the most promising way of combating the Marxist threat. Even in countries like the United States, where there was no real prospect of Marxists gaining power, the existence of a foreign Marxist enemy served to justify governments in restricting individual rights, increasing arms spending, and pursuing a bellicose foreign policy that led to the overthrow of popularly elected governments and the disastrous intervention in Vietnam.

Marx's ideas are now part of the backdrop to our thinking about society and the role played by class and economic forces. His ideas transformed the study of history and sociology, and profoundly affected philosophy, literature, and the arts. In this sense of the term we are all Marxists now.

What were the ideas that had such far-reaching effects? That is the subject of this book. But first, a little about the man from whom they came.

Origins, study, marriage

Karl Marx was born in Trier, in the German Rhineland, in 1818. His parents, Heinrich and Henrietta, came from Jewish families. Heinrich qualified as a lawyer in 1814, when the Rhineland was under French administration. After Napoleon's defeat in 1815 the Rhineland came under Prussian rule, and Jews were no longer allowed to practise law. Heinrich and his family became Lutherans, at least nominally. The family was comfortably off without being wealthy; they held liberal, but not radical, views on religion and politics.

Marx's intellectual career began badly when, at the age of 17, he went to study law at the University of Bonn. Within a year he had been imprisoned for drunkenness and slightly wounded in a duel. He also wrote love poems to his childhood sweetheart, Jenny von Westphalen. His father had soon had enough of this 'wild rampaging' as he called it, and decided that Karl should transfer to the more serious University of Berlin (see Figure 1).

1. **Karl Marx in 1836, aged 18.**

In Berlin Marx turned from law to philosophy. This did not impress his father: 'degeneration in a learned dressing-gown with uncombed hair has replaced degeneration with a beer glass,' he wrote in a reproving letter (MC 27). It was, however, the death rather than the reproaches of his father that forced Marx to think seriously about a career—for without his father's income the family could not afford to support him indefinitely. Marx therefore began work on a doctoral thesis with a view to getting a university lectureship. The thesis itself was on a remote and scholarly topic—some contrasts in the philosophies of nature of Democritus and Epicurus—but Marx saw a parallel between these ancient disputes and the debate about the interpretation of the philosophy of G. W. F. Hegel, which was at that time a meeting ground for divergent political views in German thought.

The thesis was accepted in 1841, but no university lectureship was offered. Marx became interested in journalism. He wrote on social, political, and philosophical issues for a newly founded liberal newspaper, the *Rhenish Gazette* (*Rheinische Zeitung*). His articles were appreciated and his contacts with the newspaper increased to such an extent that when the editor resigned late in 1842, Marx was the obvious replacement, even though he was only 22 years old.

Through no fault of his own, Marx's editorship was brief. As interest in the newspaper increased, so did the attentions of the Prussian government censor. A series of Marx's articles on the poverty of wine-growers in the Moselle valley may have been considered especially inflammatory; in any case, the government decided to suppress the paper.

2. Jenny Marx (neé Jenny von Westphalen).

Marx was not sorry that the authorities had, as he put it in a letter to a friend, 'given me back my liberty' (MC 50). Freed from editorial duties, he began work on a critical study of Hegel's political philosophy. He also had a more pressing concern: to marry Jenny, to whom he had now been engaged for seven years (see Figure 2). And he wanted to leave Prussia, where he could not express himself freely. The problem was that he needed money to get married, and now he was again unemployed. But his reputation as a promising young writer stood him in good stead; he was invited to become co-editor of a new publication, the *German–French Annals* (*Deutsch–Französische Jahrbücher*). This provided him with enough income to marry and also settled the question of where to go—for, as its name implies, the new publication was supposed to draw French as well as German writers and readers.

Revolutionary ideas

Karl and Jenny Marx arrived in Paris in the autumn of 1843 and soon began mixing with the radicals and socialists who congregated in this centre of progressive thought. Marx wrote two articles for the *Annals*. The publication was, however, even more short-lived than the *Rhenish Gazette* had been. The first issue failed to attract any French contributors and so was scarcely noticed in Paris, while copies sent to Prussia were confiscated by the authorities. The financial backers of the venture withdrew. Meanwhile, in view of the communist and revolutionary ideas expressed in the confiscated first issue, the Prussian government issued a warrant for the arrest of the editors. Now Marx could not return to Prussia; he was a political refugee. Luckily he received a sizeable amount of money from the former shareholders of the *Rhenish Gazette*, so he had no need of a job.

Throughout 1844 Marx worked at articulating his philosophical position. This was philosophy in a very broad sense, including politics, economics, and a conception of the historical processes at work in the world. By now Marx was prepared to call himself a communist—which was nothing very unusual in those days in Paris, where socialists and communists of all kinds could then be found.

In the same year the friendship between Marx and Engels began. Friedrich Engels (see Figure 6 on p. 51) was the son of a German industrialist who also owned a cotton factory in Manchester; but Engels had become, through contacts with the same German intellectual circles that Marx moved in, a revolutionary socialist. He contributed an article to the *Annals* that deeply affected Marx's own thinking about economics. So it was not surprising that when Engels visited Paris he and Marx should meet. Very soon they began to collaborate on a pamphlet—or rather Engels thought it was going to be a pamphlet. He left his contribution, about fifteen pages long, with Marx when he departed from Paris. The 'pamphlet' appeared under the title *The Holy Family* in 1845. Almost 300 pages long, it was Marx's first published book.

Meanwhile the Prussian government was putting pressure on the French to do something about the German communists living in Paris. An expulsion order was issued and the Marx family, which now included their first child, named Jenny like her mother, moved to Brussels.

To obtain permission to stay in Brussels, Marx had to promise not to take part in politics. He soon breached this commitment by organizing a Communist Correspondence Committee, intended to keep communists in different countries in touch with each other. Nevertheless, Marx was able to stay in Brussels for three years. He signed a contract with a publisher to produce a book consisting of a critical analysis of economics and politics. The contract called for the book to be ready by the summer of 1845. That was the first of many deadlines Marx missed for the book that was to become *Capital*. The publisher had, no doubt to his lasting regret, undertaken to pay royalties in advance of receiving the manuscript. (The contract was eventually cancelled, and the unfortunate man was still trying to get his money back in 1871.) Engels now began to help Marx financially, so the family had enough to live on.

Marx and Engels saw a good deal of each other. Engels came to Brussels, and then the two of them travelled to England for six weeks to study economics in Manchester, the heart of the new industrial age. (Meanwhile Jenny was bearing Marx their second daughter, Laura.) On his return Marx decided to postpone his book on economics. Before setting forth his own positive theory, he wanted to demolish alternative ideas then fashionable in German philosophical and socialist circles. The outcome was *The German Ideology*, a long and often turgid volume which was turned down by at least seven publishers and finally abandoned, as Marx later wrote, 'to the gnawing criticism of the mice' (P 426).

In addition to writing *The German Ideology*, Marx spent much of his time in Brussels attacking those who might have been his allies in a broader struggle against capitalism. He wrote another polemical work attacking the leading French socialist, Pierre-Joseph Proudhon. Though theoretically opposed to what he called 'a superstitious attitude to authority' (MC 157), Marx was so convinced of the importance of his own ideas that he had little tolerance for opinions different from his own. This led to frequent rows in the Communist Correspondence Committee and in the Communist League that followed it.

Marx had an opportunity to make his own ideas the basis of communist activities when he went to London in December 1847 to attend a Congress of the newly formed Communist League. In lengthy debates he defended his view of how communism would come about, and in the end he and Engels were given the task of putting down the doctrines of the League in simple language. The result was *The Communist Manifesto*, published in February 1848. It was to become the classic outline of Marx's theory.

The *Manifesto* was not, however, an immediate success. Before it could be published the situation in Europe had been transformed by the French revolution of 1848. That event triggered revolutionary movements all over Europe. The new French government revoked Marx's expulsion order, just as the nervous Belgian government gave him twenty-four hours to leave. The Marx family went first to Paris and then, following news of revolution in Berlin, returned to the Rhineland. In Cologne Marx raised money to start a radical newspaper, the *New Rhenish Gazette* (*Neue Rheinische Zeitung*). The paper supported the broad democratic movements that had made the revolution. It flourished for a time, but as the revolution fizzled out the Prussian monarchy reasserted itself and Marx was compelled to set out on his travels again. He tried Paris, only to be expelled once more; so on 24 August 1849 he sailed for England to wait until a more thoroughgoing revolution would allow him to return to the Continent.

Settling in London

Marx lived in London for the rest of his life. The family was at first quite poor. Home was two rooms in Soho. Jenny was pregnant with their fourth child (a son, Edgar, had been born in Brussels). Nevertheless, Marx was active politically with the Communist League. He wrote on the revolution in France and its aftermath, and attempted to organize support for members of the Cologne Committee of the Communist League, who had been charged by the Prussian authorities with 'treasonable conspiracy'. When the Cologne group was convicted, despite Marx's clear demonstration that the police evidence was forged, Marx decided that the League's existence was 'no longer opportune' and the League dissolved itself.

For a while Marx lived an isolated existence, unconnected with any organized political group. He spent his time reading omnivorously and engaging in doctrinal squabbles with other left-wing German refugees. His correspondence is full of complaints of being able to afford nothing but bread and potatoes

8

and little enough of those. He even applied for a job as a railway clerk, but was turned down because his handwriting was illegible. He was a regular client of the pawnshops. Yet Marx's friends, especially Engels, were generous in their gifts, and it may be that Marx's poverty was due to poor management rather than insufficient income. Jenny's maid, Helene Demuth, still lived with the family, as she was to do until Marx's death. (She was also the mother of Marx's illegitimate son, Frederick, who was born in 1851; to avoid scandal, the boy was raised by foster parents.)

These were years of personal tragedy for the family: their fourth child had died in infancy; Jenny became pregnant again, and this

3. The exterior of 41 Maitland Park Road, Haverstock Hill, London, where Marx spent the last fifteen years of his life.

child died within a year. The worst blow was the death of their son Edgar, apparently of consumption, at the age of 8.

From 1852 Marx received a steadier income. The editor of the *New York Tribune*, whom he had met in Cologne, asked him to write for the newspaper. Marx agreed, and over the next ten years the *Tribune* published an article by Marx almost every week (although some were secretly written by Engels). In 1856 the financial situation improved still further when Jenny received two inheritances. Now the family could move from the cramped Soho rooms to an eight-room house near Hampstead Heath, the scene of regular Sunday picnics for all the family (see Figure 3). In this year Marx's third daughter, Eleanor—nicknamed Tussy—was born. Although Jenny was to become pregnant one more time, the child was stillborn. From this time on, therefore, the family consisted of three children: Jenny, Laura, and Eleanor. Marx was a warm and loving father to them.

The First International and the publication of *Capital*

All this time Marx was expecting a revolution to break out in the near future. His most productive period, in 1857–8, resulted from his mistaking an economic depression for the onset of the final crisis of capitalism. Worried that his ideas would be overtaken by events, Marx began, as he wrote to Engels, 'working madly through the nights' in order to have the outlines of his work clear 'before the deluge' (MC 272). In six months he wrote more than 800 pages of a draft of *Capital*—indeed the draft is of an ambitious project that covers much more ground than *Capital* as it finally appeared. In 1859 Marx published a small portion of his work on economics under the title *Critique of Political Economy*. The book did not contain much of Marx's original ideas (except for a now famous summary of his intellectual development in the preface) and its appearance was barely noticed.

Instead of getting the remaining, more original sections of his manuscript ready for publication, Marx was distracted by a characteristic feud with a left-wing politician and editor, Karl Vogt. Marx claimed that Vogt was in the pay of the French government. Lawsuits resulted, Vogt called Marx a forger and blackmailer, and Marx replied with a 200-page book of satirical anti-Vogt polemic. Years later, Marx was shown to have been right; but the affair cost him a good deal of money and for eighteen months prevented him writing anything of lasting value.

There was also a more serious reason for Marx's tardiness in completing his work on economics. The International Workingmen's Association—later known as the First International—was founded at a public meeting in London in 1864. Marx accepted an invitation to the meeting and his election to the General Council ended his isolation from political activities. Marx's forceful intellect and strength of personality soon made him a dominant figure in the association. He wrote its inaugural address and drew up its statutes. He had, of course, considerable differences with the trade unionists who formed the basis of the English section of the International, but he showed rare diplomacy in accommodating these differences while trying constantly to draw the working-class members of the association closer to his own long-term perspective.

In 1867 Marx finally completed the first volume of *Capital*. Again, the initial reaction was disappointing. Marx's friends were enthusiastic and did what they could to get the book reviewed. Engels alone wrote seven different—but always favourable—reviews for seven German newspapers. Wider recognition came slowly. Marx became a well-known figure not because of *Capital*, but through the publication, in 1871, of *The Civil War in France*. Marx wrote this as an address to the International on the Paris Commune, the workers' uprising which, after the defeat of France at the hands of Prussia, took over and ruled the city of Paris for two months. The International had virtually nothing to do with this, but it was linked with the Commune in the popular mind. Marx's address reinforced these early suspicions of an international communist conspiracy, and Marx himself immediately gained a notoriety which, as he wrote to a friend, 'really does me good after the tedious twenty-year idyll in my den' (MC 374).

The ruthless suppression of the Commune weakened the International. Disagreements that had simmered beneath the surface now rose to the top. At the Congress of 1872, Marx found that he had lost control. A motion restricting the powers of the General Council was carried over his strong opposition. Rather than see the organization fall into the hands of his enemies, Marx proposed that the General Council should henceforth be based in New York. The motion was passed by a narrow margin. It meant, as Marx must have known it would, the end of the First International; for with communications as they then were, it was utterly impractical to run the largely European organization from across the Atlantic.

The last decade

By this time Marx was 54 years old and in poor health. The remaining ten years of his life were less eventful. Further inheritances had by now ended any threat of poverty. In many respects the Marxes' life was like that of any comfortably off bourgeois family: they lived in a large house, spent a good deal on furnishing it, sent their children to a ladies' seminary, and travelled to fashionable continental spas. Marx even claimed to have made money on the stock exchange—which did not stop him asking for, and receiving, further financial support from Engels.

Marx's ideas were spreading at last. By 1871 a second edition of *Capital* was needed. His ideas became very popular among

Russian revolutionaries, and a Russian translation of *Capital* was published in 1872. A French translation, supervised by Marx, soon followed. Although *Capital* was not translated into English during Marx's lifetime (like his other books, it was written in German) Marx's growing reputation, even among the English, was indicated by his inclusion in a series of pamphlets on 'Leaders in Modern Thought'. Marx and Engels kept up a correspondence with revolutionaries throughout Europe who shared their views. Otherwise Marx worked desultorily on the second and third volumes of *Capital*, but never got them ready for publication. That task was left, after Marx's death, to Engels. A projected fourth volume remained unwritten.

The last important work Marx wrote arose from a congress held in Gotha, a town in Germany, in 1875. The purpose of the congress was to unite rival German socialist parties, and to do this a common platform was drawn up. Neither Marx nor Engels was consulted about this platform—known as 'the Gotha Programme'—and Marx was angry at the many deviations it contained from what he considered to be scientific socialism. He wrote a set of critical comments on the Programme, and attempted to circulate it among German socialist leaders. After Marx's death this 'Critique of the Gotha Programme' was published and recognized as one of Marx's rare statements on the organization of a future communist society. At the time, however, Marx's critique had little influence, and the planned unification went ahead on the basis of a platform that was not at all in accordance with his ideas.

In his last years the satisfaction Marx might have gained from his growing reputation was overshadowed by personal sorrows. Marx's elder daughters, Jenny and Laura, married and had children, but none of Laura's three children lived beyond the age of 3. Jenny's firstborn also died in infancy, although she then had five more, all but one of whom survived to maturity. But in 1881 the older Jenny, Marx's dearly beloved wife, died after a long illness. Marx was now ill and lonely. In 1882 his daughter Jenny became seriously ill; she died in January 1883. Marx never got over this loss. He developed bronchitis and died on 14 March 1883.

Chapter 2
The young Hegelian

Hegel's *Phenomenology of Mind*

Little more than a year after Marx arrived in Berlin to study there, he wrote to his father that he was attaching himself 'ever more closely to the current philosophy' (MC 25). This 'current philosophy' was the philosophy of Hegel, who had taught at the University of Berlin from 1818 until his death in 1831 (see Figure 4). Years later, Friedrich Engels described Hegel's influence in the period when he and Marx began to form their ideas:

> The Hegelian system covered an incomparably greater domain than any earlier system and developed in this domain a wealth of thought which is astounding even today...
>
> One can imagine what a tremendous effect this Hegelian system must have produced in the philosophy-tinged atmosphere of Germany. It was a triumphal procession which lasted for decades and which by no means came to a standstill on the death of Hegel. On the contrary, it was precisely from 1830 to 1840 that 'Hegelianism' reigned most exclusively, and to a greater or lesser extent infected even its opponents.

The close attachment to this philosophy Marx formed in 1837 was to affect his thought for the rest of his life. He later described Hegel's *The Phenomenology of Mind* as 'the true birthplace and

4. G. W. F. Hegel (1770–1831) whose view of history Marx transformed.

secret of Hegel's philosophy' (*EPM* 107), so this long and obscure work is the place to begin our understanding of Marx.

The German word for 'Mind' (*Geist*) is sometimes translated as 'Spirit'. Hegel uses it to refer to the spiritual side of the universe, which appears in his writings as a kind of universal mind. My mind, your mind, and the minds of every other conscious being are particular, limited manifestations of this universal mind. There has been a good deal of debate about whether Hegel thought of this universal mind as a way of understanding the God of Christianity, or whether he was, in pantheistic fashion, identifying God with the world as a whole. There is no definite answer to this question; but it seems appropriate and convenient to distinguish this universal mind from our own particular minds by writing the universal variety with a capital, as Mind.

The Phenomenology of Mind traces the development of Mind from its first appearance as individual minds, conscious but neither self-conscious nor free, to Mind as a free and fully self-conscious unity. The process is neither purely historical, nor purely logical, but a strange combination of the two. One might say that Hegel is trying to show that history is not merely one event leading to another, but the progress of Mind following a logically necessary path, a path along which it must travel in order to reach its final goal.

The development of Mind is *dialectical*—a term that has come to be associated with Marx because his own philosophy has been referred to as 'dialectical materialism'. The dialectical elements of Marx's theory were taken from Hegel, so this is a good place to see what 'dialectic' is.

Perhaps the most celebrated passage in the *Phenomenology* concerns the relationship of a master to a slave. It well illustrates what Hegel means by dialectic, and it introduces an idea echoed in Marx's view of the relationship between capitalist and worker.

Suppose we have two independent people, aware of their own independence, but not of their common nature as aspects of one universal Mind. Each sees the other as a rival, a limit to his own power over everything else. This situation is therefore unstable. A struggle ensues, in which one conquers and enslaves the other. The master/slave relationship, however, is not stable either. Although it seems at first that the master is everything and the slave nothing, it is the slave who works and by his work changes the natural world. In this assertion of his own nature and consciousness over the natural world, the slave achieves satisfaction and develops his own self-consciousness, while the master becomes dependent on his slave. For Hegel, the ultimate outcome must therefore be the liberation of the slave, and the overcoming of the initial conflict between the two independent beings.

This is only one short section of the *Phenomenology*, the whole of which traces the development of Mind as it overcomes contradiction or opposition. Mind is inherently universal, but in its limited form, as the minds of particular people, it is not aware of its universal nature—that is, particular people do not see themselves as all part of the one universal Mind. Hegel describes this as a situation in which Mind is 'alienated' from itself—people (who are manifestations of Mind) take other people (who are also manifestations of Mind) as something foreign, hostile, and external to themselves, whereas they are in fact all part of the same all-encompassing whole.

Mind cannot be free in an alienated state, for in such a state it appears to encounter opposition and barriers to its own complete development. Since Mind is really infinite and all-encompassing, the opposition and barriers are only appearances, the result of Mind not recognizing itself for what it is, but taking what is really a part of itself as something alien and hostile to itself. These apparently alien forces limit the freedom of Mind, for if Mind does not know its own infinite powers it cannot exercise these powers to organize the world in accordance with its plans.

The progress of the dialectical development of Mind in Hegel's philosophy is always progress towards freedom. 'The History of the World is none other than the progress of the consciousness of freedom,' he wrote. The *Phenomenology* is thus an immense philosophical epic, tracing the history of Mind from its first blind groping in a hostile world to the moment when, in recognizing itself as master of the universe, it finally achieves self-knowledge and freedom.

This vision of world history has an odd consequence that would have been embarrassing to a more modest author. If all history is the story of Mind working towards the goal of understanding its own nature, this goal is finally achieved with the completion of the *Phenomenology* itself. When Mind, manifested in the mind of

Hegel, grasps its own nature, the culminating stage of Mind's progress towards freedom has been reached, and history has therefore run its course. Hegel thus saw himself as standing at the end of history.

To us this seems preposterous. Hegel's speculative mixture of philosophy and history has been unfashionable for a long time. When Marx was young, however, it was taken very seriously.

How the Young Hegelians transformed Hegel

To understand Marx, it is important to recognize that we can make sense of much of the *Phenomenology* even if we reject the notion of a universal Mind as the ultimate reality of all things. We can treat 'Universal Mind' as a collective term for all human minds. We can then rewrite the *Phenomenology* in terms of the path to human liberation. The saga of Mind then becomes the saga of humanity's progress towards freedom.

In the decade following Hegel's death, a group of philosophers known as Young Hegelians attempted just such a reinterpretation of Hegel's thought. The orthodox interpretation of Hegel was that since human society is the manifestation of Mind in the world, everything is right and rational as it is. There are plenty of passages in Hegel's works that can be quoted in support of this view. At times Hegel even seems to regard the Prussian state as the supreme incarnation of Mind. Since the Prussian state paid his salary as a professor of philosophy, it is not surprising that the more radical Young Hegelians took the view that in these passages Hegel had betrayed his own ideas. Among these was Marx, who wrote in his doctoral thesis: 'if a philosopher really has compromised, it is the job of his followers to use the inner core of his thought to illuminate his own superficial expressions of it' (D 17).

For the Young Hegelians the 'superficial expression' of Hegel's philosophy was his acceptance of the state of politics, religion, and society in early 19th-century Prussia. The 'inner core' was his account of Mind overcoming alienation, reinterpreted as an account of human self-consciousness freeing itself from the illusions that prevent it achieving self-understanding and freedom.

Marx, during his student days in Berlin and for a year or two afterwards, was close to Bruno Bauer, a lecturer in theology and a leading Young Hegelian. Under Bauer's influence Marx seized on orthodox religion as the chief illusion standing in the way of human self-understanding. The chief weapon against this illusion was philosophy. In the Preface to his doctoral thesis, Marx wrote:

> Philosophy makes no secret of it. The proclamation of
> Prometheus ... (in a word, I detest all the gods)—is her own
> profession, her own slogan against all the gods of heaven and
> earth who do not recognize man's self-consciousness as the
> highest divinity. There shall be none other beside it.   (D 17)

In accordance with the general method of the Young Hegelians, Bauer and Marx used Hegel's own critique of religion to reach more radical conclusions. In the *Phenomenology* Hegel referred to the Christian religion at a certain stage of its development as a form of alienation, for while God reigns in heaven, human beings inhabit an inferior and comparatively worthless 'vale of tears'. Human nature is thus seen as divided between its essence, which is immortal and heavenly, and its non-essential, mortal, and earthly incarnation. Hence individuals see themselves as fulfilled only after they leave their body and enter another realm; they are alienated from their mortal existence and the world in which they actually live.

Hegel, treating this as a passing phase in the self-alienation of Mind, drew no practical conclusions from it. Bauer reinterpreted it more broadly as indicating the self-alienation of human beings. It was humans, he maintained, who had created this God that now seemed to have an independent existence, an existence that made it impossible for humans to regard themselves as 'the highest divinity'. This philosophical conclusion pointed to a practical task: to criticize religion and show human beings that God is their own creation, thus ending the subordination of humanity to God and the alienation of human beings from their own true nature. The Young Hegelians were captivated by Hegel's philosophy, but regarded it as mystifyingly presented and incomplete. To make sense of it, it needed to be rewritten in terms of the material world instead of the mysterious world of Mind. They reinterpreted 'Mind' to mean 'human self-consciousness'. The goal of history then became the liberation of humanity; but this could not be achieved until the religious illusion had been overcome.

Chapter 3
From God to money

Feuerbach's critique of religion

Ludwig Feuerbach carried through, more forcefully than Bruno
Bauer, the transformation of Hegel's method into a weapon
against religion.

Friedrich Engels later wrote of the impact of the work that
made Feuerbach famous: 'Then came Feuerbach's *Essence
of Christianity* ... One must himself have experienced the
liberating effect of this book to get an idea of it. Enthusiasm was
general; we all became at once Feuerbachians.' Like Bauer,
Feuerbach characterized religion as a form of alienation. God,
he wrote, is to be understood as the essence of the human
species, externalized and projected into an alien reality.
Wisdom, love, benevolence—these are really attributes of
the human species, but we attribute them, in a purified form,
to God. The more we enrich our concept of God in this way,
however, the more we impoverish ourselves. The solution is to
realize that theology is a kind of misdescribed anthropology.
What we believe of God is really true of ourselves. Thus humanity
can regain its essence, which in religion it has lost.

When *The Essence of Christianity* appeared, in 1841, the first
meeting between Marx and Engels still lay two years ahead.

The book may not have made as much of an impression on Marx as it did on Engels, for Marx had already been exposed, through Bauer, to similar ideas; but Feuerbach's later works, particularly his *Preliminary Theses for the Reform of Philosophy*, did have a decisive impact on Marx, triggering off the next important stage in the development of his thought.

Feuerbach's later works went beyond the criticism of religion to the criticism of Hegelian philosophy itself. Yet it was a curious form of criticism of Hegel, for Feuerbach continued to work by transforming Hegel, using Hegel's method against all philosophy in the Hegelian mode. Hegel had taken Mind as the moving force in history, and humans as manifestations of Mind. This, according to Feuerbach, locates the essence of humanity outside human beings and thus, like religion, serves to alienate humanity from itself.

More generally, Hegel and other German philosophers of the idealist school began from such conceptions as Spirit, Mind, God, the Absolute, the Infinite, and so on, treating these as ultimately real, and regarding ordinary humans and animals, tables, sticks and stones, and the rest of the finite, material world as a limited, imperfect expression of the spiritual world. Feuerbach reversed this, insisting that philosophy must begin with the finite, material world. Thought does not precede existence: existence precedes thought.

So Feuerbach put at the centre of his philosophy neither God nor thought, but man. Hegel's tale of the progress of Mind, overcoming alienation in order to achieve freedom, was for Feuerbach a mystifying expression of the progress of human beings overcoming the alienation of both religion and philosophy itself.

The economic turn

Marx seized on this idea of bringing Hegel down to earth, and he too began using Hegel's methods to attack the present material and economic condition of human beings. In his brief spell as editor of the *Rhenish Gazette*, Marx had descended from the rarefied air of Hegelian philosophy to more practical issues like censorship, divorce, a Prussian law prohibiting the gathering of dead timber from forests, and the economic distress of Moselle wine-growers. When the paper was suppressed Marx went back to philosophy, applying Feuerbach's technique of transformation to Hegel's political philosophy, but with a greater awareness of the social and economic problems faced by ordinary people.

Marx's ideas at this stage (1843) are liberal rather than socialist, and he still thinks that a change in consciousness is all that is needed to improve social conditions. In a letter to Arnold Ruge, a fellow Young Hegelian with whom he worked on the short-lived *German–French Annals*, Marx wrote: 'Freedom, the feeling of man's dignity, will have to be awakened again in these men. Only this feeling…can again transform society into a community of men to achieve their highest purposes, a democratic state.' And in a later letter to Ruge about their joint venture:

> we can summarize the tendency of our journal in one word: self-understanding (equals critical philosophy) by our age of its struggles and wishes. This is a task for the world and for us. It can only be the result of united forces. What is at stake is a confession, nothing more. To get its sins forgiven, humanity only needs to describe them as they are.   (R 45)

Up to this point Marx had followed Feuerbach in reinterpreting Hegel as a philosopher of man rather than Mind. His view of human beings, however, focused on their mental aspect, their thoughts, and their consciousness. The first signs of a shift to his later emphasis on the material and economic conditions of human life came in an essay written in 1843 entitled 'On the Jewish Question'. The essay reviews two publications by Bruno Bauer on the issue of civil and political rights for Jews.

Marx rejects his friend's treatment of the issue as a question of religion. It is not the sabbath Jew we should consider, Marx says, but the everyday, secular Jew. Accepting the common stereotype of Jews as obsessed with money and bargaining, Marx describes the Jew as merely a special manifestation of what he calls 'civil society's Judaism'—that is, the dominance in society of bargaining and financial interests generally. Marx therefore suggests that the way to abolish the 'problem' of Judaism is to reorganize society so as to abolish money and the bargaining that follows from it.

If Marx were our contemporary, we would be shocked that he does not question the fairness or accuracy of the view, widely accepted in Europe in his time, that Jews are more concerned with money or bargaining than other people. Perhaps, in a society in which antisemitism was widespread, he was anxious not to draw attention to his own Jewish origins. Whatever the reason, the essay shows a lack of sensitivity to the issue of antisemitism, but it does not show, as some have suggested, that Marx himself was an antisemite. Marx's purpose was not to discuss 'the Jewish question' as a general social issue, but to use it as an illustration of how society should be reformed. In terms of the development of Marx's thought, the importance of the essay is that for the first time, Marx sees economic life, not religion, as the chief form of human alienation. Another German writer, Moses Hess, had already developed Feuerbach's ideas in this direction, being the first, as Engels put it, to reach communism by 'the philosophic path'. (There had, of course, been many earlier communists who were more or less philosophical—what Engels meant was the path of *Hegelian* philosophy.) Now Marx was heading down the same path, following Feuerbach's example of transforming Hegel in order to show how human freedom can be achieved. The following quotation from 'On the Jewish Question' reads exactly like Bauer, Feuerbach, or Marx himself, a year or two earlier,

denouncing religion—except that where they would have
written 'God' Marx now substitutes 'money':

> Money is the universal, self-constituted value of all things. It has
> therefore robbed the whole world, human as well as natural, of its
> own values. Money is the alienated essence of man's work and
> being, this alien essence dominates him and he adores it.   (J 67–8)

The final sentence points the way forward. First the Young
Hegelians, including Bauer and Feuerbach, see religion as the
alienated human essence, and seek to end this alienation through
their critical studies of Christianity. Then Feuerbach goes beyond
religion, arguing that any philosophy that concentrates on the
mental rather than the material side of human nature is a form
of alienation. Now Marx insists that it is neither religion nor
philosophy, but money that is the barrier to human freedom.
The obvious next step is a critical study of economics. This Marx
now begins.

Before we follow this development, however, we must pause
to note the emergence of another key element in Marx's work that,
like economics, was to remain central to his thought and activity.

Chapter 4
Enter the proletariat

Philosophy's material weapon

We saw that when the Prussian government suppressed the newspaper Marx had been editing, he started work on a critique of Hegel's political philosophy. In 1844 he published, in the *German–French Annals*, an article entitled 'Towards a Critique of Hegel's *Philosophy of Right*: Introduction'. The critique that this article was to introduce was not published until after Marx's death, but the 'Introduction' stands alongside 'On the Jewish Question' as a milestone on the road to Marxism. For it is in this article that Marx first allocates to the working class a decisive role in the coming redemption of humanity.

The 'Introduction' starts by summarizing the attack on religion made by Bauer and Feuerbach. This passage is notable for its epigrams, especially the frequently quoted description of religion as 'the opium of the people'. That phrase is usually understood simply as an attack on religion, but read in context, it suggests a more nuanced idea: 'Religion is the sigh of the oppressed creature, the heart of a heartless world, and the soul of soulless conditions. It is the opium of the people.' Marx portrays religion as a response to the oppression and heartlessness of the world; but an inadequate response because instead of challenging the oppression itself, it merely numbs the pain.

The introduction continues along familiar lines, saying that human self-alienation has been unmasked in its holy form, and now it is the task of philosophy to unmask it in its unholy forms, such as law and politics. Marx calls for more criticism of German conditions, to allow the German people 'not even a moment of self-deception'. But for the first time—and in contrast to Bauer and Feuerbach—Marx suggests that criticism by itself is not enough:

> The weapon of criticism cannot, of course, supplant the criticism of weapons; material force must be overthrown by material force. But theory, too, will become material force as soon as it seizes the masses. (I 77)

In his initial recognition of the role of the masses, Marx treats this role as a special feature of the German situation, not applicable to France. Perhaps because France had already had two revolutions—from 1789 to 1799 and again in 1830—Marx writes that there 'every class of the nation is *politically idealistic* and experiences itself first of all not as a particular class but as representing the general needs of society'. In Germany, on the other hand, practical life is 'mindless' and no class can be free until it is forced to be 'by its *immediate* condition, by *material* necessity, by its *very chains*'. Where then, Marx asks, is the positive possibility of German freedom to be found? And he answers:

> in the formation of a class with radical chains... a sphere that has a universal character because of its universal sufferings... a sphere that... is the complete loss of humanity and thus can only recover itself by a complete redemption of humanity. This dissolution of society, as a particular class, is the proletariat. (I 81)

In ancient Rome, the lowest class of citizens was the proletariat. Marx applies this term to industrial society to refer to the working class, those who do not own property and live by selling their labour. In his transformation of Hegelian philosophy, he now finds a crucial role for this class: 'As philosophy finds in the proletariat its material weapons, so the proletariat finds in philosophy its intellectual weapons.' He then puts it more explicitly: 'Philosophy cannot realize itself without transcending the proletariat, the proletariat cannot transcend itself without realizing philosophy' (I 81–2).

Here is the germ of a new solution to the problem of human alienation. Criticism and philosophical theory alone will not end it. A more practical force is needed, and that force is provided by the artificially impoverished working class. This lowest class of society will 'realize philosophy'—by which Marx means the culmination of the philosophical and historical saga described, in a mystified form, by Hegel. The proletariat, following the lead of the new radical philosophy, will complete the dialectical process in which humans have emerged, grown estranged from themselves, and become enslaved by their own alienated essence. The property-owning middle class could win freedom for themselves, but in doing so, they would not win freedom for all human beings. In maintaining their own property rights, they would be excluding others from the freedom they gain. The propertyless working class, however, possess nothing but their status as human beings, and thus can liberate themselves only by liberating all humanity.

Before 1844, to judge from his writings, Marx scarcely noticed the existence of the proletariat; certainly he never suggested that the working class had a part to play in overcoming alienation. Now, like a film director calling on the errand-boy to play Hamlet, Marx introduces the proletariat as the material force that will bring about the liberation of humanity—thus taking over the part played by Hegel himself, in his vision of Mind achieving freedom by becoming conscious of its own universal nature.

The dialectical role of the proletariat

Marx did not arrive at his view of the proletariat as the result of detailed economic studies. His economic studies were just beginning. He had read a great deal of history, but he does not buttress his position by quoting from historical sources, as he was later to do. His reasons for placing importance on the proletariat are philosophical rather than historical, economic, or scientific. Since human alienation is not a problem of a particular class, but a universal problem, whatever is to solve it must have a universal character—and the proletariat, Marx claims, has this universal character in virtue of its total deprivation. It represents not a particular class of society, but all humanity.

That a situation should contain within itself the seed of its own dissolution, and that the greatest of all triumphs should come from the depths of despair—these are familiar themes in the dialectic of Hegel and his followers. They echo, some have said, the redemption of humanity by the crucifixion of Jesus, and it is not difficult to see parallels between Hegel's famous master/slave dialectic, and Marx's dialectic of the capitalist ruling class and the proletariat. The proletariat fits neatly into this dialectical scenario, and one cannot help suspecting that Marx seized upon it precisely because it served his philosophical purposes so well. After all, the work in which he first bestows this role on the proletariat is an introduction to a critique of Hegel's philosophy.

To say this is not to say that when Marx wrote the 'Introduction' he knew nothing about the proletariat. He had just moved to Paris, where socialist ideas were much more advanced than in Germany. He mixed with socialist leaders of the time, living in the same house as one of the leaders of the League of the Just, a radical workers' group. His writings reflect his admiration of the French socialist workers: 'The nobility of man', he writes, 'shines forth upon us from their toil-worn bodies' (MC 79). In giving so important a role to the proletariat, therefore, the 'Introduction' reflects a two-way process: Marx tailors his conception of the proletariat to suit his philosophy, and tailors his philosophy in accordance with his new-found enthusiasm for the working class and its revolutionary potential.

Chapter 5
The first Marxism

A critique of economics

Marx had now developed two important new ideas. The first is that the chief form of human alienation is not philosophical nor religious, but economic, grounded in the way we satisfy our material wants; and the second is that the material force needed to liberate humanity from its domination by the capitalist system lies in the working class. Up to this stage, however, Marx had made these points only briefly, in essays ostensibly on other topics. Marx's next step was to use these ideas as the basis of a new and systematic world-view, one that would transform and supplant the Hegelian system and all prior transformations of it.

Marx began his critical study of economics in 1844. It was to culminate in his greatest work, *Capital: A Critique of Political Economy*, the first volume of which was published in 1867, with later volumes appearing after Marx's death. So the work Marx produced in Paris, known as the *Economic and Philosophic Manuscripts of 1844*, was the initial instalment of a project that was to occupy him, in one form or another, for the rest of his life.

The 1844 version of Marxism was not published until 1932. The manuscript consists of a number of disconnected sections, some obviously incomplete. Nevertheless, we can see what Marx was trying to do. He begins with a Preface that praises Feuerbach as the author of the only writings 'since Hegel's *Phenomenology* and *Logic* to contain a real theoretical revolution' (*EPM* 30). There are then sections on the economics of wages, profits, and rent, in which Marx quotes liberally from the founding fathers of classical economics like J.-B. Say and Adam Smith. The point of this, as Marx explains, is to show that according to classical economics the worker becomes a commodity, the production of which is subject to the ordinary laws of supply and demand. If the supply of workers exceeds the demand for labour, wages fall and some workers starve. Wages therefore tend to the lowest possible level compatible with keeping an adequate supply of workers alive.

Marx draws another important point from the classical economists. Those who employ the workers—the capitalists—build up their wealth through the labour of their workers. They become wealthy by keeping for themselves a certain amount of the value their workers produce. Capital is nothing else but accumulated labour. The worker's labour increases the employer's capital. This increased capital is used to build bigger factories and buy more machines. More sophisticated machinery increases the division of labour, thus putting more self-employed workers out of business. Now the formerly self-employed workers have no option but to sell their labour on the market. This intensifies the competition among workers trying to get work, and lowers wages.

All this Marx presents as deductions from the presuppositions of orthodox economics. Marx himself is not writing as an economist. He wants to rise above the level of the science of economics, which, he says, simply takes for granted such things as private property, greed, competition, and so on, saying nothing about the extent to which apparently accidental circumstances are really the expression of a necessary course of development. Marx wants to ask larger questions, ignored by economists, such as 'What in the evolution of mankind is the meaning of this reduction of the greater part of mankind to abstract labour?' (By 'abstract labour'

Marx means work done simply in order to earn a wage, rather than for the worker's own specific purposes. Thus making a pair of shoes because one wants a pair of shoes is not abstract labour; making a pair of shoes because that happens to be a way of getting money is.) Marx, in other words, wants to give a deeper explanation of the meaning and significance of the laws of economics.

Alienated labour

What type of explanation does Marx have in mind? The answer is apparent from the section of the manuscripts entitled 'Alienated Labour'. Here Marx explains the implications of economics in terms that consciously parallel Feuerbach's critique of religion:

> the more the worker externalizes himself in his work, the more powerful becomes the alien, objective world that he creates opposite himself, the poorer he becomes himself in his inner life and the less he can call his own. It is just the same in religion. The more man puts into God, the less he retains in himself. The worker puts his life into the object and this means that it no longer belongs to him but to the object...The externalization of the worker in his product implies not only that his labour becomes an object, an exterior existence but also that it exists outside him, independent and alien, and becomes a self-sufficient power opposite him, that the life that he has lent to the object affronts him, hostile and alien. (*EPM* 81)

The central point is more pithily stated in a sentence preserved in the notebooks Marx used when studying the classical economists, in preparation for the writing of the 1844 manuscripts: 'We can see how economics rigidifies the alienated form of social intercourse, as the essential, original form that corresponds to man's nature' (M 126).

This is the gist of Marx's objection to classical economics. Marx examines economics from a perspective that is broader and more historically grounded than that taken by classical economists. Whereas economics rests on presupposing private property, competition, and individuals who single-mindedly pursue personal enrichment, Marx argues that these phenomena are to be found only in a particular condition of human existence, a condition of alienation. In contrast to Hegel, whom Marx praises for grasping the self-development of man as a historical process, the classical economists take the present alienated condition of human society as its 'essential, original and definitive form'. They fail to see that it is a necessary but temporary stage in the evolution of mankind.

Next, Marx turns to the present alienated state of humanity. One of his premises is that 'man is a species-being'. The idea is taken directly from Feuerbach who in turn derived it from Hegel. Hegel, as we saw, told the story of human development in terms of the progress of a single Mind, of which individual human minds are particular manifestations. Feuerbach scrubbed out the super-Mind, and rewrote Hegel in less mysterious human terms; but he retained the idea that human beings are in some sense a unity. For Feuerbach the basis of this unity, and the essential difference between humans and animals, is the ability of humans to be conscious of their species. It is because they are conscious of their existence as a species that human beings can see themselves as individuals (that is, as one among others), and it is because humans see themselves as a species that human reason and human powers are unlimited. Human beings partake in perfection—which, according to Feuerbach, they mistakenly attribute to God instead of themselves—because they are part of a species.

Marx transforms Feuerbach, making the conception of man as a species-being still more concrete. For Marx, 'productive life is species-life' (*EPM* 90). It is in activity, in production, that humans show themselves to be species-beings. In support of this claim, Marx points out that while animals produce only to satisfy their immediate needs, and in preset ways, as a spider weaves a web, human beings can produce according to universal standards. They can create things for which they have no immediate need, bounded only by the limits of their imagination and their sense of beauty.

On this view, labour in the sense of free productive activity is the essence of human life. Whatever is made in this way—a statue, a house, or a piece of cloth—is therefore the essence of human life made into a physical object. Marx calls this 'the objectification of the species-life of man' (*EPM* 91). Ideally the objects workers have freely created would be theirs to keep or dispose of as they wish. Under conditions of alienated labour, workers must produce objects over which they have no control, because the products of their labour belong to their employers. The employers then sell these objects, profiting from their sale, and increasing their capital. In this way the workers' products are used to increase the wealth and power of the employers. Thus the workers are alienated from the products of their labour. They are also alienated from their activity, because they have sold their labour-time to capitalists, who control them and compel them to work long hours of repetitive, mindless factory work. Because workers are no longer able to produce freely in accordance with their imagination—and that was, Marx thought, what distinguishes us from non-human animals—workers are alienated from their species-being.

These three ways in which workers are alienated—from the products of labour, from their activity, and from their species-being—lead to a fourth. For workers, productive activity becomes 'activity under the domination, coercion and yoke of another man'—the capitalist employer. This other human being becomes an alien, hostile being. Instead of humans relating to each other cooperatively, they relate competitively. Love and trust are replaced by bargaining and exchange. Human beings cease to recognize in each other their common human nature; instead they see others as instruments for furthering their own egoistic interests. They are alienated from their common humanity.

That, in brief, is Marx's first critique of economics. Since in his view it is economic life rather than Mind or consciousness that is ultimately real, this critique is his account of what is really wrong with the present condition of humanity. The next question is: What can be done about it?

Marx rejects the idea that anything would be achieved by an enforced wage rise. Labour for wages is not free productive activity. It is merely a means to an end. Marx describes higher wages as nothing but 'a better payment of slaves' that does nothing to restore significance or dignity to workers (*EPM* 93). Instead, Marx advocates the abolition of wages, alienated labour, and private property in one blow: in a word, communism. He introduces communism in terms befitting the closing chapter of a Hegelian epic:

> Communism...is the genuine solution of the antagonism between man and nature and between man and man. It is the true solution of the struggle between existence and essence, between objectification and self-affirmation, between freedom and necessity, between individual and species. It is the solution to the riddle of history and knows itself to be this solution.   (*EPM* 97)

One might expect Marx to go on and explain in some detail what communism would be like. He does not—in fact despite the vital importance that communism has in his philosophy, nowhere in his writings does he give more than sketchy suggestions about what a communist society would be like. He does, however, gesture at the enormous difference communism would make. All human senses, he claims, are degraded by private property. The dealer in minerals sees the market value of the jewels he handles, not their beauty. In the alienated condition caused by private property we cannot appreciate anything except by possessing it, or using it as a means. The abolition of private property will liberate our senses from this alienated condition, and enable us to appreciate the world in a truly human way. Just

as the musical ear perceives a wealth of meaning and beauty
where the unmusical ear can find none, so will the senses of
social human beings differ from those of the unsocial.

The significance of 'the first Marxism'

These are the essential points of 'the first Marxism'. It is manifestly
not a scientific enterprise, at least not in the sense in which we
understand science today. Its theories are not derived from
detailed observations or factual studies, nor subjected to
controlled tests or observations.

The first Marxism is more down to earth than Hegel's philosophy
of history, but it is still a speculative philosophy of history rather
than a scientific study. The aim of world history is human freedom.
Human beings are not now free, for they are unable to organize
the world so as to satisfy their needs and develop their human
capacities. Private property, though a human creation, dominates
and enslaves human beings. Ultimate liberation, however, is not
in doubt; it is philosophically necessary. The immediate task of
revolutionary theory is to understand in what way the present
situation is a stage in the dialectical progress to liberation. Then
it will be possible to encourage the movements that will end the
present stage, ushering in the new age of freedom.

Marx's writings after 1844—including all the works which made
him famous—are reworkings, modifications, developments,
and extensions of the themes of the *Economic and Philosophic
Manuscripts*. The number and bulk of these writings make it
impossible to discuss each work adequately. (Their repetitiveness
would also make it extremely tedious.) So from here on I shall
depart slightly from a strict chronological account. I shall begin
by tracing the development of the materialist conception of
history, which Marx himself described as the 'guiding thread for
my studies' (P 425), and Engels, in his funeral oration by Marx's
grave, hailed as Marx's chief discovery, comparable with Darwin's

discovery of the theory of evolution. This will occupy Chapters 6 and 7. In Chapter 8 I shall consider Marx's economic works, principally, of course, *Capital*. Since *Capital* was written only after Marx had arrived at the materialist conception of history, the departure from chronological order in these chapters will be slight. It will be greater in Chapter 9, the last of these expository chapters, which will assemble from passages of varying vintage Marx's thoughts on communism, revolution, and on the ethical principles underlying his preference for a communist rather than a capitalist form of society.

Chapter 6
The development of the materialist theory of history

The Holy Family

Marx's first published book—and, incidentally, the first work in which Engels participated—attacked articles published in the *General Literary Gazette* (*Allgemeine Literatur-Zeitung*), a journal edited by Marx's former friend and teacher, Bruno Bauer. Since Bauer's brother was a co-editor, the book was mockingly entitled *The Holy Family*. The best comment on it was made by Engels: 'the sovereign derision that we accord to the *General Literary Gazette* is in stark contrast to the considerable number of pages that we devote to its criticism'. Nevertheless, some passages of *The Holy Family* are interesting because they show Marx in transition between the *Economic and Philosophic Manuscripts* and later statements of the materialist conception of history.

One section is a defence of the French socialist Proudhon and his objections to private property. Marx is still thinking in terms of alienation:

> The propertied class and the class of the proletariat present the same human self-alienation. But the former class finds in this self-alienation its confirmation and its good, its own power: it has in it a semblance of human existence. The class of the proletariat

feels annihilated in its self-alienation; it sees in it its own
powerlessness and the reality of an inhuman existence. (*HF* 148)

Then comes a passage in which the outlines of an embryonic
materialist theory of history are clearly visible:

> Indeed private property, too, drives itself in its economic movement
> towards its own dissolution, only, however, through a development
> which does not depend on it, of which it is unconscious and which
> takes place against its will, through the very nature of things; only
> inasmuch as it produces the proletariat as proletariat, that misery
> conscious of its spiritual and physical misery, that dehumanization
> conscious of its dehumanization and therefore self-abolishing...The
> question is not what this or that proletarian, or even the whole
> of the proletariat at the moment considers as its aim. The question
> is what the proletariat is, and what, consequent on that being, it will
> be compelled to do. Its aim and historical action is irrevocably and
> obviously demonstrated in its own life situation as well as in the
> whole organization of bourgeois society today. (*HF* 149)

The structure of this and surrounding passages is Hegelian. Private
property and the proletariat are described as 'antitheses'—the two
sides of a Hegelian contradiction. It is a necessary contradiction,
one that could not have been otherwise, for private property
cannot maintain its own existence without also maintaining the
existence of the propertyless working class needed to run the
factories. The proletariat, on the other hand, is compelled by its
miserable situation to seek to abolish itself, which is something
it cannot do without the abolition of private property. The end
result will be that both private property and the proletariat
'disappear', or, in Hegelian terminology, are transcended in a
new synthesis that resolves the previous contradiction.

Here we have an early version of the materialist theory of history.
The basis of the dialectical movement Marx describes is not the
hopes and plans of people, but the economic imperatives that flow

from the existence of private property. The proletariat becomes conscious of its misery, and therefore seeks to overthrow the capitalist form of society, but this consciousness arises only because of the present situation of the proletariat in society. Marx and Engels make this point more explicitly in a famous sentence in *The German Ideology*: 'Life is not determined by consciousness, but consciousness by life' (*GI* 181).

The 'Theses on Feuerbach'

According to Engels's later account of the relationship between German philosophy and the materialist conception of history, 'the first document in which is deposited the brilliant germ of the new world outlook' is not *The Holy Family* but the 'Theses on Feuerbach' which Marx jotted down in the spring of 1845. These 'Theses' consist of eleven brief remarks in which Marx distinguishes his own form of materialism from that of Feuerbach. Their epigrammatic form has caused them to become among the most quoted of Marx's writings, but because Engels published them in 1888, long before any of Marx's other early unpublished writings appeared, they are also among the most misunderstood.

Despite Engels's accolade, the 'Theses' largely recapitulate points Marx had made before. They attack Feuerbach and earlier materialists for taking a passive view of objects and our perception of them. Idealists like Hegel and Fichte emphasized that our activities shape the way we see the world. They were thinking of mental activity. A child sees a red ball, rather than a flat red circle, only when the child has mentally grasped the idea of three-dimensional space. Marx wants to combine the active, dialectical side of idealist thought with the materialism of Feuerbach: hence 'dialectical materialism' as later Marxists called it (though Marx himself never used this phrase).

By the active side of materialism Marx meant the practical human activity that he thought was needed to solve theoretical problems.

We have seen examples of this. In 'On the Jewish Question' Marx wrote that the problem of the status of Jews, which Bauer had seen as a problem in religious consciousness, would be abolished by reorganizing society so as to abolish bargaining. In 'Towards a Critique of Hegel's *Philosophy of Right*: Introduction', Marx argued that philosophy cannot be realized without the material weapon of the proletariat. And in the *Economic and Philosophic Manuscripts* Marx had referred to communism as 'the riddle of history solved'. This 'riddle of history' is Hegel's riddle of how Mind is to achieve liberation. In Marx's transformation the contradictions Hegel describes in *The Phenomenology of Mind* become contradictions in the human condition. They can only be resolved by communism.

The 'Theses on Feuerbach' are the principal source of the celebrated Marxist doctrine of 'the unity of theory and practice'. Some think of this unity as discussing Marxist philosophy during quiet moments on the barricades. Others take it as meaning that one should live in accordance with one's values—the challenge encapsulated in the title of a book by the Canadian philosopher Gerald Cohen: *If You're an Egalitarian, How Come You're So Rich?* The intellectual context of the 'Theses' makes it clear that Marx had neither of these ideas in mind. For Marx the unity of theory and practice meant the resolution of theoretical problems by practical activity. It is an idea that makes little sense outside the context of a materialist transformation of Hegel's philosophy of world history.

The eleventh thesis on Feuerbach is engraved on Marx's tombstone in Highgate Cemetery. It reads: 'The philosophers have only interpreted the world in various ways; the point is, to change it' (T 173) (see Figure 5 and Figure 12 on p. 116) . This is generally read as a statement to the effect that philosophy is unimportant; revolutionary activity is what matters. It means nothing of the sort. What Marx is saying is that the problems of philosophy cannot be solved by mere interpretation of the world

5. The manuscript of Marx's 11th Thesis on Feuerbach.

as it is, but only by remoulding the world to resolve the
philosophical contradictions inherent in it. Philosophy is crucial
because it points to the problems that can be overcome only by
changing the world.

The German Ideology

The materialist conception of history is a theory of world history
in which practical human activity, rather than thought, plays
the crucial role. The most detailed statement of the theory is to
be found in Marx and Engels's next major work, *The German
Ideology* (1846). Like *The Holy Family* this was a polemic
of inordinate length against rival thinkers. Marx later wrote that
the book was written 'to settle our accounts with our erstwhile
philosophical conscience' (P 426).

This time Feuerbach is included in the criticism, although treated
more respectfully than the others. It is in the section on Feuerbach
that Marx and Engels take the opportunity to state their new
view of world history:

> The first premise of all human history is, of course, the existence of
> living human individuals...Men can be distinguished from animals
> by consciousness, by religion, or anything else you like. They
> themselves begin to distinguish themselves from animals as soon as
> they begin to produce their means of subsistence, a step which is

43

conditioned by their physical organization. By producing their means of subsistence men are indirectly producing their actual material life...In direct contrast to German philosophy which descends from heaven to earth, here we ascend from earth to heaven. That is to say, we do not set out from what men say, imagine, conceive, nor from men as narrated, thought of, imagined, conceived, in order to arrive at men in the flesh. We set out from real, active men, and on the basis of their real life-process we demonstrate the development of the ideological reflexes and echoes of this life-process. The phantoms formed in the human brain are also, necessarily, sublimates of their material life-process, which is empirically verifiable and bound to material premises. Morality, religion, metaphysics, all the rest of ideology and their corresponding forms of consciousness, thus no longer retain the semblance of independence. They have no history, no development; but men, developing their material production and their material intercourse, alter, along with this, their real existence, their thinking, and the products of their thinking. Life is not determined by consciousness, but consciousness by life.   (*GI* 176–7, 180–1)

This is as clear a statement of the broad outline of his theory as Marx was ever to achieve. Thirteen years later, summing up the 'guiding thread' of his studies, he used similar language: 'It is not the consciousness of men that determines their being, but, on the contrary, their social being that determines their consciousness' (P 425). With *The German Ideology* we have arrived at Marx's mature formulation of the outline of historical materialism (though not the detailed account of the process of change).

In view of this, and Marx's later description of the work as settling accounts with his 'former philosophic conscience', it might be thought that Marx's early interest in alienation has now been replaced by a more scientific approach. It has not. Henceforth, Marx makes more use of historical data and less use of abstract philosophical reasoning about the way the world must be; but his interest in alienation persists. *The German Ideology* still describes social power as something which is really nothing other than the productive force of individuals, and yet appears to these individuals as 'alien and outside them' because they do not understand its origin and cannot control it. Instead of them directing it, it directs them. The abolition of private property and the regulation of production under communism would abolish this 'alien relation between men and what they themselves produce' and enable men to 'get exchange, production, the mode of their mutual relation, under their own control again' (*GI* 186).

It is not the use of the word 'alienation' that is important here. The same point can be made in other words. What is important is that Marx's theory of history is a vision of human beings in a state of alienation. Human beings cannot be free if they are subject to forces that determine their thoughts, their ideas, their very nature as human beings. The materialist conception of history tells us that human beings are subject to forces they do not understand and cannot control. These forces are not supernatural tyrants, forever above and beyond human control, but the productive powers of human beings themselves. These productive powers, instead of serving human beings, appear to them as alien and hostile forces. The description of this state of alienation, along with the more detailed explanation of its origins and the form it takes, is the materialist conception of history.

Chapter 7
The goal of history

What does the materialist theory of history really tell us?

We have now traced the development of the materialist conception of history from its origins in Marx's early concern with human freedom and alienation, but we have yet to examine the details of this theory of history. Is it really, as Engels claimed, a scientific discovery of 'the law of development of human history', comparable to Darwin's discovery of the law of development of organic nature?

The classic formulation of the materialist conception of history is the one Marx gives in the Preface to *A Contribution to the Critique of Political Economy*, written in 1859. We have already seen a little of this summary by Marx of his own ideas, but it merits a lengthier quotation:

> In the social production of their life, men enter into definite relations that are indispensable and independent of their will, relations of production which correspond to a definite stage of development of their material productive forces. The sum total of these relations of production constitutes the economic structure of society, the real foundation, on which rises a legal and political superstructure and to which correspond definite forms of social

consciousness. The mode of production of material life conditions the social, political, and intellectual life process in general. It is not the consciousness of men that determines their being, but, on the contrary, their social being that determines their consciousness. At a certain stage of their development, the material productive forces of society come in conflict with the existing relations of production, or—what is but a legal expression for the same thing—with the property relations within which they have been at work hitherto. From forms of development of the productive forces these relations turn into their fetters. Then begins an epoch of social revolution. With the change of the economic foundations the entire immense superstructure is more or less rapidly transformed. In considering such transformations a distinction should always be made between the material transformation of the economic conditions of production, which can be determined with the precision of natural science, and the legal, political, religious, aesthetic, or philosophic—in short, ideological forms in which men become conscious of this conflict and fight it out.   (P 425-6)

It is commonly said that Marx divided society into two elements, the 'economic base' and the 'superstructure', and maintained that the base governs the superstructure. A closer reading of the passage just quoted reveals a threefold, rather than a twofold, distinction. The opening sentence refers to relations of production, corresponding to a definite stage of the material powers of production. Thus we start with powers of production, or 'productive forces', as Marx usually calls them. Productive forces are things used to produce. They include labour-power, raw materials, and the machines available to process them. If a miller uses a handmill to grind wheat into flour, the handmill is a productive force. The productive forces give rise to relations of production. Relations of production are relations between people, or between people and things. The miller may own his mill, or may rent it from its owner. *Owning* and *renting* are relations of production. Relations between people, such as 'Smith employs Jones' or 'Ramsbottom is the serf of the Earl of Warwick', are also relations of production. It is these relations—not the forces themselves—that constitute the economic structure of society. This economic structure, in turn, is the foundation on which the superstructure rises.

So the materialist conception of history starts with productive forces. Marx says that relations of production correspond to the stage of development of productive forces. In one place he puts this very bluntly: 'The handmill gives you society with the feudal lord; the steam mill, society with the industrial capitalist' (*PP* 219–20).

In other words, when the productive forces are developed only to the stage of manual power, the typical relation of production is that of lord and serf. This and similar relations make up the economic structure of society, which in turn is the foundation of the political and legal superstructure of feudal times. Along with laws giving kings certain rights over their subjects, and lords rights over their serfs, a feudal society will have the kind of religion and morality that goes with such a society: an authoritarian and hierarchically organized religion that preaches a morality based on concepts of loyalty, obedience, and fulfilling the duties of one's station in life, no matter how low it may be.

According to this view of history, feudal relations of production came about because they fostered the development of the productive forces of feudal times—the handmill for example—but these productive forces were not static. They continued to develop. The steam mill was invented. The most efficient use of steam power is in large factories which require a concentration of free labourers. Feudal relations of production restrict the ability of serfs to leave the land. So the productive relation of lord and serf breaks down, to be replaced by the productive relation of capitalist and employee. These new relations of production now constitute the new economic structure of society, on which a capitalist legal and political superstructure rises, with its own law, religion, and morality. Freedom of contract and freedom of movement become legal rights, along with the freedom to dispose of one's property. The privileges of the landed nobility are whittled away, and individual rights, including freedom of conscience, are increasingly recognized, along with greater acceptance of competitiveness and the pursuit of self-interest.

So we have a three-stage process: productive forces determine relations of production, which in turn determine the political, legal, and ideological superstructure. The productive forces are fundamental. Their growth provides the momentum for the whole process of history.

Problems of interpretation

Should we take seriously the statement about the handmill giving us feudal lords, and the steam mill capitalists? Surely Marx must have realized that the invention of steam power depended on human ideas, and those ideas, as much as the steam mill itself, have produced capitalism. Isn't Marx deliberately stating his theory in a crude and exaggerated form in order to display its novelty?

This is a vexed question. The passage about the handmill and the steam mill is not the only one in which Marx says flatly that productive forces determine everything else. There are several others; but there are also statements in which Marx acknowledges the causal contribution of factors belonging to the superstructure. Particularly when Marx writes about historical events—for instance in *The Eighteenth Brumaire of Louis Bonaparte*, in which Marx describes the events of 1851–2 in France that enabled Louis Bonaparte, the nephew of Napoleon I, to seize power—Marx traces the effects of ideas and personalities, and makes comments that seem incompatible with the determinism of the view that everything is determined by the development of productive forces. Thus in *The Eighteenth Brumaire*, Marx writes:

> Men make their own history, but they do not make it just as they please; they do not make it under circumstances chosen by themselves, but under circumstances directly encountered, given, and transmitted from the past. (*EB* 329)

Then there is the famous opening declaration of *The Communist Manifesto*: 'The history of all hitherto existing society is the history of class struggles' (*CM* 246). If productive forces determine everything, class struggles can be no more than the superficial form in which these forces play out. Like the images on a cinema screen they would reflect the underlying reality, but be powerless to change it. So why describe history as the history of class struggles? And if neither thought nor politics has any real causal significance, what is the point of Marx's political activity for the working class, or of the rallying call with which Marx and Engels bring to a close the *Communist Manifesto* (and still to be seen engraved on his tombstone in Highgate Cemetery, as shown in Figure 12, on p. 116): 'Workers of all lands, unite!'?

After Marx died, Engels denied that Marx had said that 'the economic element is the *only* determining one'. He and Marx, he conceded, were partly to blame for this misinterpretation, for they had emphasized the economic side in opposition to those who rejected it altogether. Marx and he had not, Engels wrote, overlooked the existence of interaction between the economic structure and the rest of the superstructure. They had affirmed only that 'the economic movement finally asserts itself as necessary'. According to Engels, Marx grew so irritated at misinterpretations of his doctrine that towards the end of his life, he declared: 'All I know is that I am not a Marxist.'

Was Engels right? Some have accused him of watering down the true doctrine; yet no one was in a better position to know what

Marx really meant than his lifelong friend and collaborator. Moreover the 20th-century publication of Marx's *Grundrisse*—a rough preliminary version of *Capital* and other projects Marx never completed—reveals that Marx did, like Engels, use such phrases as 'in the last analysis' to describe the predominance of the economic elements in the interacting whole that constitutes human existence (*G* 495). Right or wrong, one cannot help sympathizing with Engels's position after Marx died. As the authoritative interpreter of Marx's ideas he had to present them in a plausible form, a form not refuted by Marx's other writings, nor by common-sense observations about the effect of politics, religion, or law on the productive forces (see Figure 6).

6. Friedrich Engels (1820–95), Marx's friend, co-author, and financial supporter.

But once 'interaction' between the superstructure and the productive forces is admitted, is it still possible to maintain that production determines the superstructure, rather than the other way round? It seems that we then face the old chicken-and-egg problem all over again. The productive forces determine the relations of production to which correspond the ideas of the society. These ideas lead to the further development of productive forces, which lead to new relations of production, to which correspond new ideas. In this cyclical movement it makes no more sense to say that productive forces play the determining role than to say that the egg ensures the continued existence of chickens, rather than the other way round.

Talk of the productive forces 'finally' or 'in the last analysis' determining the other interacting factors does not provide a way out of the dilemma. For what can this mean? Does it mean that in the end the superstructure is totally governed by the development of the forces of production? In that case 'finally' merely stretches the causal chain; it is still a chain and so we are back with the hard-line determinist version of the theory.

On the other hand, if 'finally' not merely stretches, but actually breaks, the chain of economic determinism, it is difficult to see that asserting the primacy of the productive forces can mean anything significant. It might mean, as the passage from *The German Ideology* quoted in Chapter 6 appears to suggest, that the process of human history only gets going when humans 'begin to produce their means of subsistence'; or as Engels put it in his graveside speech: 'mankind must first of all eat, drink, have shelter and clothing, before it can pursue politics, science, art, religion, etc.' But if politics, science, art, and religion, once they come into existence, have as much effect on the productive forces as the productive forces have on them, the fact that mankind must eat first and can only pursue politics afterwards is of historical interest only. Art has been found going back 60,000 years. No doubt the artists had to eat, drink, and find

shelter before they carved their designs into the rock walls of their caves. But how does that fact help us to understand the causal process that led to capitalism, let alone that by which it will be overthrown?

Alternatively, describing the economic side as 'finally' asserting itself could be an attempt to say that although both economic and non-economic factors interact, a larger proportion of the causal impetus comes from the productive forces. But on what basis could one say this? How could one divide the interacting processes and say which played the larger role? One way of understanding this is in terms of probability. We might say, for example, that when different political or religious forces are struggling for supremacy, those that will foster the development of productive forces, and advance the interests of the class that will benefit most from that development, have an advantage and, more often than not, will come out on top. To say this is not to say that the political or religious struggles make no difference. Occasionally the tactics used by one side will be decisive, overwhelming the economic factors; but not often.

The goal of history

A scientific discovery?

If we interpret the materialist conception of history as hard-line economic determinism, that would indeed, if it were true, be a momentous discovery, but does not seem to be true. If we instead appeal to the much more pliable conception to be found in the *Grundrisse*, where Marx describes society as a 'totality', an 'organic whole' in which everything is interconnected, we interpret Marx as saying no more than that society is an interconnected totality (*G* 99–100). That conception is illuminating when set against the view that ideas, politics, law, religion, and so on have a life and history of their own, independently of mundane economic matters. Nevertheless it does not amount to 'the law of development of human history', or to a scientific discovery comparable to Darwin's theory of evolution.

Between these two extremes lies the probability conception just sketched. On that view, when struggles take place at the level of the ideological superstructure, the ideas and institutions that favour the development of the forces of production, and the interests of the class that will benefit from the development of those forces, are likely to prevail. Could that claim qualify as a scientific discovery? One way of answering this is to ask if it is precise enough to enable us to deduce from it certain consequences rather than others. That is how we test proposed scientific laws—by seeing if the consequences they predict actually occur. The probability conception of the materialist interpretation of history is difficult to test, because it is not possible to find a large number of similar ideological struggles, determine in advance in each case which side is better aligned with the development of productive forces and the interests of the class that will gain from that development, and then see whether that side wins in a statistically significant majority of cases. It may be more realistic for advocates of the probability conception to claim only that, in analysing such struggles, it will be useful to ask whether one side or the other is more likely to allow the productive forces to develop fully, and to benefit from that development. We can then explore the influence of these factors on the outcome of the struggle. On this view, the materialist conception of history suggests directions for research, and that research may develop more specific testable hypotheses. The materialist conception of history will then stand or fall by how fruitful these suggestions, and any testable hypotheses they generate, turn out to be. That is a controversial question, but many social scientists consider that Marx's suggestions have been very fruitful indeed.

It still needs to be explained how Marx, though obviously aware of the effect of the superstructure on the productive forces, could so confidently and—at least sometimes—bluntly assert that the productive forces determine the relations of production and hence the social superstructure. Why did he not see the difficulty posed

by the existence of interaction? Is the explanation simply that, as Engels suggested, Marx overstated his case for polemical purposes?

That is one possible explanation, but there could also be a deeper one: that belief in the primacy of the productive forces was not, for Marx, an ordinary belief about a matter of fact but a legacy of the origin of his theory in Hegelian philosophy. One way to see this is to ask why, if Marx's view is inverted Hegelianism, the existence of interaction between ideas and material life does not pose exactly the same problem for Hegel's view (that the progress of Mind determines material life) as it poses for Marx's inversion of this view. Hegel's writings contain as many descriptions of material life influencing consciousness as Marx's contain of consciousness influencing material life. (The master/slave dialogue is an example, as we saw in Chapter 2.) So the problem of establishing the primary causal role of one set of factors over the other should be as great for Hegel as for Marx.

Hegel's reason for believing in the primacy of consciousness is clear: he regards Mind as ultimately real, and the material world as a manifestation of it; accordingly, he sees the purpose or goal of history as the liberation of Mind from all illusions and fetters. Hegel's belief that consciousness determines material life therefore rests on his view of ultimate reality and the meaning of history. History is not a chain of meaningless and often accidental occurrences, but a necessary process heading towards a discoverable goal. Whatever happens on the stage of world history happens in order to enable Mind to reach its goal. It is in this sense that what happens on the level of Mind, or consciousness, is the *real* cause of everything else.

Like Hegel, Marx has a view about what is ultimately real. His materialism is the reverse of Hegel's idealism. The materialist conception of history is usually regarded as a theory about the causes of historical change, rather than a theory about the nature of ultimate reality. In fact it is both—as Hegel's idealist conception of history was both. We have already seen passages from *The German Ideology* indicating that Marx took material processes as real in a way that ideas are not. There Marx and Engels contrast the 'real life-process' of 'real, active men' with 'the ideological reflexes and echoes of this life-process'. They distinguish the 'phantoms formed in the human brain' from the 'material life-process, which is empirically verifiable'. The frequent reiteration of 'real' or 'actual' in describing the material or productive life of human beings, and the use of words like 'reflex', 'echo', 'phantom', and so on for aspects of consciousness, suggest that Marx and Engels are making a philosophical distinction between what is real and what is merely a manifestation or appearance.

Nor is this terminology restricted to Marx's early works. The contrast between appearance and reality is repeated in *Capital*, where the religious world is said to be merely the 'reflection' of the real world (*C* I 73).

Marx takes from Hegel the idea that history is a necessary process heading towards a discoverable goal. We have seen evidence of this in the *Economic and Philosophic Manuscripts*, where Marx criticized classical economists for saying nothing about the meaning of economic phenomena 'in the evolution of mankind' or about the extent to which 'apparently accidental circumstances' are nothing but 'the expression of a necessary course of development'. This too is not a view limited to Marx's youthful period, as shown by, for instance, the following paragraph from an article he wrote in 1853 for the *New York Daily Tribune*, entitled 'The British Rule in India':

> England, it is true, in causing a social revolution in Hindustan, was actuated only by the vilest interests, and was stupid in her manner of enforcing them. But that is not the question. The question is, can mankind fulfil its destiny without a fundamental revolution in the

social state of Asia? If not, whatever may have been the crimes of England, she was the unconscious tool of history in bringing about that revolution.

The references to 'mankind's destiny' and to England as 'the unconscious tool of history' imply that history moves in a purposive way towards some goal. (The passage is reminiscent of Hegel's account of how 'the cunning of reason' uses unsuspecting individuals to work its purposes in history.)

Marx's idea of the goal of world history was, of course, different from Hegel's. He replaced the liberation of Mind by the liberation of real human beings. Instead of seeing history as the development of Mind through various forms of consciousness to final self-knowledge, Marx saw it as the development of human productive forces, by which human beings free themselves from the tyranny of nature and fashion the world after their own plans. But for Marx the progress of human productive forces is no less necessary, and no less progress towards a goal, than the progress of Mind towards self-knowledge is for Hegel.

We can now explain the primary role of the productive forces in Marx's theory of history in the same manner as we explained Hegel's opposite conviction: for Marx the productive life of human beings, rather than their ideas and consciousness, is ultimately real. The development of these productive forces, and the liberation of human capacities that this development will bring, is the goal of history.

Marx's suggestion about England's role in bringing humanity closer to its destiny illustrates the nature of the primacy of material life. Since England's colonial policy involves a series of political acts, if this policy leads to a social revolution in Asia, that would be an instance of the superstructure affecting the economic base. This happens, though, in order to develop the productive forces to the state necessary for the fulfilment of human destiny.

The superstructure acts only as the 'unconscious tool' of history. England's colonial policy is no more the ultimate cause of the social revolution in Asia than my spade is the ultimate cause of the growth of my vegetables.

If this interpretation is correct the materialist theory of history is no ordinary causal theory. Few historians—or philosophers for that matter—now see any purpose or goal in history. They do not explain history as the necessary path to anywhere. They explain it by showing how one set of events brought about another. Marx, in contrast, saw history as the development of the real nature of human beings, that is, human beings satisfying their wants and exerting their control over nature by their productive activities. The materialist conception of history was not conceived as a modern scientific account of how economic changes lead to changes in other areas of society. It was conceived as an explanation of history which points to the real forces operating in it, and the goal to which these forces are heading.

That is why, while recognizing the effect of politics, law, and ideas on the productive forces, Marx was in no doubt that the development of the productive forces determines everything else. This also makes sense of Marx's dedication to the cause of the working class. Marx was acting as the tool—in his case, a fully conscious tool—of history. The productive forces always finally assert themselves, but they do so through the actions of individual humans who may or may not be conscious of the role they are playing in history.

A popular joke asks how many Marxists it takes to change a lightbulb, and answers 'None. The lightbulb contains the seeds of its own revolution.' That suggests a question we might have asked Marx, if we had had the opportunity: 'Since you believe that the productive forces will finally assert themselves, why did you bother to spend so many evenings going to meetings of the International Workingmen's Association, rather than relaxing at home with your family?' Marx might have answered that he enjoyed being the tool of history. More reasonably, he might have believed that although the productive forces would finally assert themselves anyway, the transition to the new communist era would come sooner if he helped the workers to get organized—and since capitalism causes so much unnecessary suffering, the sooner it is replaced, the better.

Chapter 8
Economics

Tracing the development of Marx's economics

Marx regarded *Capital* as his masterpiece. In it, he presented his economic theories to the public in their most finished form. 'Most finished', not 'finished'; Marx saw only the first volume of *Capital* through to publication. After Marx's death, Engels assembled the second and third volumes from materials Marx had left behind, and a fourth volume, entitled *Theories of Surplus Value*, was prepared by Karl Kautsky, a Czech-Austrian socialist theorist.

As with the materialist conception of history, so with the economics: the mature form is easier to appreciate in the light of earlier writings. So let us return to Marx's ideas in 1844, the point at which we ceased to follow their general development and went off in pursuit of the materialist conception of history.

By 1844 Marx had come to hold that the capitalist economic system, regarded by the classical economists as natural and inevitable, was an alienated form of human life. Under capitalism workers are forced to sell their labour—which Marx regards as the essence of human existence—to the capitalists, who use this labour to accumulate more capital, which further increases the power of the capitalists over the workers. Capitalists become rich, while wages are driven down to the bare minimum needed to keep the workers alive. Yet in reducing so large a class of people to this degraded condition, capitalism creates the material force that will overthrow it. For Marx, the importance of economics lay in the explanation it provided of the workings of this alienation and the manner in which it could be overcome.

In the years immediately after 1844 Marx's major literary efforts went into polemical works: *The Holy Family*, *The German Ideology*, and *The Poverty of Philosophy*. In the course of castigating his opponents Marx developed the materialist conception of history, but did not greatly advance his economic theories. His first attempt to work out these theories in any detail came in 1847, when he gave a series of lectures on economics to the Workingmen's Club in Brussels. The lectures were revised and published as newspaper articles in 1849, and later reprinted under the title *Wage-Labour and Capital*, a lucidly written work, containing many echoes of the 1844 manuscripts, but without their Hegelian terminology. It is worth examining in some detail, because its clarity makes the more difficult *Capital* easier to grasp.

Marx starts with labour. Labour is described as 'the worker's own life-activity, the manifestation of his own life'. Yet it becomes, under capitalism, a commodity the worker must sell in order to live. Therefore his life-activity is reduced to a means to go on living. It is not part of his life, but 'a sacrifice of his life'. His real life only begins when his work ceases, 'at table, in the public house, in bed' (*WLC* 275–6).

Marx then asks how wages are determined and answers that the price of labour is determined like the price of any other commodity. It may rise or fall according to supply and demand, but the general tendency is for wages to level down to the cost of production of labour, that is, a subsistence wage that pays no more than what is necessary in order to keep the worker alive and capable of working and reproducing.

Next Marx turns to capital. He states the view of English classical economics, that capital consists of the raw materials, instruments of production, and means of subsistence which are used in further production. Since all these elements of capital are the creation of labour, even the classical economists hold that capital is accumulated labour.

What the classical economists overlook, however, is that all this is true only within a certain set of social relations. Just as a person of African descent is not, as such, a slave, but can become a slave in a slave-owning society, so accumulated labour becomes capital only in bourgeois society.

The classical economists see capital as natural, rather than socially conditioned, because they see it as material products—machines, raw materials, etc. These material products, however, are also commodities. Commodities are items which can be exchanged against other items—for instance, a pound of sugar may be exchangeable for two pounds of potatoes, or half a pound of strawberries. They therefore have exchange-value. 'Exchange-value' is a key term in Marxist economics. It is contrasted with 'use-value'. The use-value of a pound of sugar is its power to satisfy people's desires for something sweet. The exchange-value of a pound of sugar might be, in a certain time and place, two pounds of potatoes or, expressed in terms of money, say, £1. Use-values therefore exist independently of a market or any other system of exchange: exchange-values do not.

Now capital is really a sum of commodities, that is, of exchange-values. Whether it consists of wool, cotton, machines, buildings, or ships, it remains capital. While all capital is a sum of exchange-values, however, not all sums of exchange-values are capital. A sum of exchange-values becomes capital only if used to increase itself by being exchanged for labour. Thus capital cannot exist without hiring wage-labour. Nor can wage-labour exist unless hired by capital. This is the basis of the claim made by bourgeois economists that the interests of the capitalists and the workers are one and the same.

Marx now examines this 'much-vaunted community of interests between worker and capitalist'. He takes the case most favourable for the bourgeois economists, the situation in which capital is growing, and hence the demand for labour, and the price of labour, is rising.

Marx's first point is one still made by critics of the modern consumer society:

> A house may be large or small; as long as the surrounding houses are equally small it satisfies all social demands for a dwelling. But let a palace arise beside the little house, and it shrinks from a little house to a hut...however high it may shoot up in the course of civilization, if the neighbouring palace grows to an equal or even greater extent, the occupant of the relatively small house will feel more and more uncomfortable, dissatisfied and cramped within its four walls. (*WLC* 284)

Poverty and affluence are affected by the wealth of our neighbours because, Marx says, our desires are of a social nature. They are produced by our life in society, rather than by the desired objects in themselves. Thus even steadily rising wages do not produce greater satisfaction if the standard of living of the capitalist has risen even more—and this is exactly what happens when the growth of capital produces a rise in wages. Growth in capital means a growth in profit, but Marx claims this can only happen if the relative share of wages is reduced. In this, Marx is following the respected classical economist David Ricardo. Wages may rise in real terms, but the gulf between workers and capitalists will increase.

Marx also describes a more fundamental opposition between capitalists and workers. If capital grows, the domination of capital over workers increases. Wage-labour 'produces the wealth of others that rules over it' (*WLC* 284). From this hostile power the labourers receive their means of subsistence, only on the condition that they again assist the further growth of capital.

Capital increases its domination by increasing the division of labour. This occurs because competition between capitalists forces them to make labour ever more productive, and the greater the scale on which they can produce, and the greater the division of labour, the more productive labour is. This increasing division of labour has several effects.

First, it enables one worker to do the work of ten, and so increases the competition among workers for jobs, thus driving wages down.

Second, it simplifies labour, eliminates the special skills of the worker, and transforms him into 'a simple, monotonous productive force' (*WLC* 291).

Third, it puts more small-scale capitalists out of business. They can do nothing but join the working class. 'Thus', says Marx, 'the forest of uplifted arms demanding work becomes ever thicker, while the arms themselves become ever thinner' (*WLC* 293).

Finally, Marx says, as the scale of production increases and new markets are needed to dispose of the production, economic crises become more violent. Initially a crisis of overproduction can be relieved by opening up a new market or more thoroughly exploiting an old one. This room for manoeuvre shrinks as production expands. *Wage-Labour and Capital* closes with an image of capitalism collapsing into its grave, but taking with it the corpses of its slaves, the workers, who perish in economic crises.

And all this, Marx ironically reminds us, when capital is growing—the most favourable condition for wage-labour!

Wage-Labour and Capital contains no answer to a crucial puzzle common to classical economists like Ricardo and Marx in his own early theory. Both held that commodities are, on average, exchanged for their value. They also held a 'labour theory of value', namely the theory that the exchange-value of a commodity corresponds to the amount of labour it takes to produce it. (Value is, Marx was later to write, 'crystallized social labour' (VPP 31).) But labour is a commodity too. Like other commodities, it should, on average, be exchanged for its value. The capitalist who buys a day's labour should therefore, on average, have to pay the value of a day's labour. This will add the value of a day's labour to the production cost of the commodity the worker produces in that day. This commodity the capitalist will then sell for a price that, on average, corresponds to the value of the labour required to produce it. Where then does the capitalist get his profit from?

We know from the *Grundrisse*—the rough draft of *Capital* and other related projects—that Marx first worked out his solution to this puzzle in 1857–8.

The most intriguing point about the *Grundrisse* is that although it was written well into Marx's maturity, it is closer, in both terminology and method of argument, to the 1844 *Manuscripts* than to any of the works published in Marx's lifetime after 1844. Even if it were not possible to trace transformed Hegelian themes in the works of Marx's mature period published during his lifetime, the *Grundrisse* makes it plain that Marx did not make the decisive break with Hegelian philosophy that his reference to *The German Ideology* as 'settling accounts with our former philosophic conscience' has commonly been taken to imply.

The key element of Marx's mature economic theory appears in the *Grundrisse*. The worker, Marx writes:

> sells labour itself as *objectified labour*; i.e. he sells labour only in so far as it already objectifies a definite amount of labour, hence in so

far as its equivalent is already measured, given; capital buys it as living labour as the general productive force of wealth; activity which increases wealth.   (*G* 307)

What does Marx mean by this distinction between objectified and living labour? Objectified labour is the predetermined amount for which the capitalist pays—for instance, the worker's labour for one day. This is labour as a commodity. The exchange-value of this commodity is the amount needed to produce it, that is, the amount needed to keep the worker alive and reproducing, so that there will be a continuous supply of labour. But there is a dual nature to the exchange of labour and capital. The capitalist obtains the use of the worker's labour-power for the prescribed period—say, one day—and can use this labour-power to produce as much wealth as he is able to get out of it. This is what Marx means when he says that capital buys 'living labour'. The worker gets a fixed sum, regardless of what the capitalist can make out of the worker's labour-power.

Surplus value

At Marx's funeral, Engels said that the second of Marx's great discoveries was 'the discovery of surplus value'. Surplus value is the value the capitalist is able to extract from the labour-power he buys, above the exchange-value that he must pay for it. It is the difference between labour-power as a creative, productive force, and labour-time as an objectified commodity.

Suppose that the cost of keeping a worker alive and reproducing for one day is £1, and suppose that a day's work consists of twelve hours. Then the exchange-value of twelve hours' labour will be £1. Fluctuations above this figure will be short-lived, because competition for work from the unemployed will keep driving it down. Suppose, however, that the development of the forces of production means that a worker's labour-power can be used to add £1 to the value of some raw materials in only six hours. Then the

7. The round reading room of the old British Library, opened in 1842, where Marx worked on *Capital*.

worker effectively earns his wages in six hours. But the capitalist has bought twelve hours of labour-power for his £1, and can now use the remaining six hours to extract surplus value from the worker. This is, Marx claims, the secret of how capital is able to use the worker's creative power to increase its domination over the worker.

Marx published some of his new economic ideas in 1859, in *A Critique of Political Economy*. This work is justifiably famous for the succinct summary of the materialist view of history contained in its Preface, which we discussed in Chapter 7; but the economic ideas were insignificant compared with those published eight years later in the first volume of *Capital*. So we shall go straight on to this pinnacle of Marx's writings. (See Figure 7.)

Capital

Capital has a familiar-sounding subtitle—*A Critique of Political Economy*—and once again the work criticizes classical economic theories, both from within their own presuppositions and from a broader point of view. But *Capital* also contains historical material on the origin of capital, and detailed descriptions, drawn from government publications like the reports of factory inspectors, of the horrific nature of factory labour. We can see how all this fits in with Marx's general theoretical system by examining the first chapter of *Capital*, on commodities, and particularly the final section of this chapter, intriguingly entitled 'The Fetishism of the Commodity and its Secret'.

According to Marx, commodities are mysterious things in which the social character of human labour appears to be an objective feature of the product of that labour. He illustrates this by commenting that to religious believers the productions of the human brain seem to be independent beings. Similarly, with commodities, a social relation between human beings appears in the form of the value of a commodity, as if that value were objective and independent of human relations. Like religious believers bowing before an idol, we make a fetish of commodities by treating them as more than they really are.

How does this happen? It happens only when we begin to produce things not because they directly serve our wants, but in order to exchange them. Since the exchange-value of a product corresponds to the amount of labour required to produce it, when we produce in order to exchange, the value of our labour becomes its exchange-value, rather than its use-value. When we exchange our products we are, without being aware of it, taking as equal the different kinds of labour embedded in them.

In a society based on the production of commodities there is, Marx says, a 'mystical veil' over these 'life-processes of society' which would not exist if we produced 'as freely associated men', consciously regulating our production in a planned way (*C* I 173). Then the value of a product would be its use-value, the extent to which it satisfies our desires. Classical economists like Adam

Smith and David Ricardo lifted the veil far enough to see that the value of a product (i.e. its exchange-value) represents the labour-time it took to produce it; but they took this as a law of nature, a self-evident necessary truth. On the contrary, says Marx, it bears the stamp of a society 'in which the process of production has the mastery over man, instead of the opposite' (*C* I 175).

The aim of *Capital*, then, is to rip aside this mystical veil over the life-processes of modern society, revealing these processes as the domination of human beings by their own social relations. Thus *Capital*, like Marx's other writings, is based on the idea that human beings are in a state of alienation, a state in which their own creations appear to them as alien, hostile forces and in which instead of controlling their creations, they are controlled by them.

Within this overall conception, the details of *Capital* fall into place. The economic theory, contained mostly in the first nine chapters, is an attempt to display the real economic basis of production in a capitalist society. Here Marx debates with the classical economists, trying to show that, even on their own terms, he has a better account of the economic workings of capitalism than they do.

Most of these first nine chapters prepare the ground for, and then introduce, the notion of surplus value. This involves a lengthy restatement, in plain language, of the point made in more Hegelian terms in the *Grundrisse*. The dual nature of commodities, which can be seen as use-values or exchange-values, affects labour too. What is special about labour, though, is that it is the measure of exchange-value. Thus a new machine that makes it possible to produce two coats in the time it used to take to produce one will increase the use-value of an hour's labour (because two coats are more useful than one) but will not increase the exchange-value of the hour's labour (because an hour's labour remains an hour's labour, and if a coat can be made in only half the time it used to take, it will, in the end, be worth correspondingly less). Increasing the fruitfulness of labour therefore increases its use-value but not the exchange-value of its output.

This is how capitalism enslaves its workers. Through machinery and the division of labour, capitalism greatly increases the productivity of human labour; but this increased productivity does not benefit the producers. If in pre-capitalist times people had to work for twelve hours to produce the necessities of life, doubling the productivity of their labour ought to mean that they can now choose between an extra six hours of leisure, twice as many useful products, or some combination of the two. Under capitalism, however, labour is geared to the production of goods for exchange. Paradoxically, under these conditions increased productivity does not lead to the production of more exchange-value. Instead, the exchange-value per item of what is produced drops. Small independent producers are forced to become wage-labourers, since they cannot produce as many items in a day as the larger producers who obtain economies of scale by the use of wage-labourers. Since wages tend to fall to a subsistence level, the overwhelming majority of human beings gain nothing from the increased productivity of human labour. That, at any rate, is Marx's view.

But what happens to the increased productivity, if it does not improve the lives of the workers? Marx's answer is that it is skimmed off from the worker's output in the form of surplus value. The capitalist obtains the use-value of the worker's labour-power, and pays only the exchange-value. Because labour-power is a commodity that can be used to produce more value than it has itself, the capitalist is able to retain the difference between the two.

The fact that the worker obtains only the exchange-value, rather than the use-value, of his labour, means that in order to earn enough to support himself he has to work a full day—say, twelve hours—whereas his labour produces the use-values of the necessary food, clothing, shelter, and so on in, say, six hours. Marx calls the six hours in which the worker produces the value of the goods he needs 'socially necessary labour-time' because it is labour that the worker would have to undertake in any economic system, given the level of development of forces of production. The extra six hours are surplus labour, which Marx regards as a form of forced labour for the benefit of the capitalist (*C* I 129). The essential difference between a society based on slave-labour and one based on wage-labour lies, Marx says, only in the veiled manner in which this surplus labour is extracted from the real producer, the worker.

The significance of all this lies in the fact that Marx regards the hours people must work to keep themselves alive as hours in which they are not free: 'The realm of freedom really begins only where labour determined by necessity and external expediency ends' (*C* III 958–9).

In primitive societies property was held in common. People were not alienated from each other, or from the products of their labour, but at the same time human productive forces were so poorly developed that people had to spend much of their time providing for their needs, and for all that time were not free to choose what to do. The growth of the forces of production led to a feudal form of society in which the serf was subordinate to the feudal lord, and had to work a specified number of days on the lord's land rather than on his own. It was then perfectly obvious when the serf was working to feed himself and when he was working for his lord. At neither time was he free to choose his own activity.

The vastly greater development of productive forces that takes place under capitalism provides the means, Marx believes, to reduce the domination of nature over us to insignificant proportions. This huge increase in productivity should make it possible to hugely increase human freedom. Under capitalism, however, this potential increase in human freedom cannot become actual for the majority of the population, because the position of workers as a class in relation to capitalists as a class means that they are not free. They must take the terms the capitalists offer them, or starve; and capitalists will only employ them under terms that allow surplus value to be extracted from their labour. This is not because capitalists are cruel or greedy—though some may be—but because of the economic laws inherent in capitalist production which, through free competition, coerce individual capitalists just as they coerce individual workers. (Although capitalists and workers are equally coerced, capitalists suffer far less from this coercion than workers.)

Marx sums all this up:

> Capitalism also developed into a coercive relation, and this compels the working class to do more work than would be required by the narrow circle of its own needs. As an agent in producing the activity of others, as an extractor of surplus labour and exploiter of labour-power, it surpasses all earlier systems of production, which were based on directly compulsory labour, in its energy and its quality of unbounded and ruthless activity. (*C* I 424–5)

The most gripping chapters of *Capital* are not those in which Marx expounds his economic theories, but those which record the consequences of capitalist efficiency. The tenth chapter, on 'The Working Day', chronicles the capitalists' attempts to squeeze more and more labour-time out of the workers, oblivious to the human costs of working 7-year-old children for fifteen hours a day. The struggle for a legally limited working day is, Marx writes, more vital to the working classes than a pompous catalogue of 'the inalienable rights of man' (*C* I 416). Other chapters describe how the increasing division of labour eliminates intellectual and manual skill and reduces the labourer to a mere appendage to a machine; how industrialization has ruined cottage industries, forcing hand-workers to starve; how capitalism creates an 'industrial reserve army' of unemployed workers, subsisting in the direst poverty, to keep the 'active army of workers' in check; and how the agricultural population of England had their land taken from them by landlords and capitalists, so that they could survive only by selling their labour-power (*C* I 792). The documented evidence presented justifies Marx's description of capital as 'dripping from head to toe, from every pore, with blood and dirt' (*C* I 926). (See Figure 8.)

Near the end of the first volume of *Capital* the gloom lifts. Marx sketches how the laws of capitalism will bring about its own destruction. On the one hand competition between capitalists will lead to an ever-diminishing number of monopoly capitalists: on the other hand the 'misery, oppression, slavery, degradation, and exploitation' of the working class will continue to grow. But the working class is, because of the nature of capitalist production, more numerous and better organized. Eventually the dam will burst. The ensuing revolution will be, says Marx, lapsing into the style of his earlier writings, 'the negation of the negation' (*C* I 929). It will not mean a return to private property in the old sense, but to property based on the gains made under capitalism, that is,

8. An English factory during the industrial revolution.

on cooperation and common possession of land and the means of production. Capitalism will make the transition relatively easy, since it has already expropriated all private property into its own hands. All that is now necessary is for the mass of the people to expropriate these few expropriators.

The second and third volumes of *Capital* are much less interesting than the first. The second volume is written from the perspective of circulation, rather than production, and is largely a technical discussion of how capital circulates. It also discusses the origin of economic crises. The third volume attempts to patch up some problems in the first volume, particularly the objection that prices do not reflect the amount of labour in a product, as one would expect them to do on Marx's account. More important is Marx's claim that under capitalism the rate of profit tends to fall. Marx argued that the surplus value of the past accumulates in the form of capital. Hence capital is always increasing, and the ratio of 'living labour' to capital is always decreasing; but since capitalists only make profit by extracting surplus value from living labour, this means that the rate of profit must fall in the long run. All this was part of Marx's attempt to show that capitalism cannot be a permanent state of society.

How to think about Marx's critique of capitalism

Marx, Engels, and later Marxists treat *Capital* as a contribution to the science of economics. In those terms it is open to several damning objections. For instance, Marx asserts that all profit arises from the extraction of surplus value from living labour; machines, raw materials, and other forms of capital cannot generate profit, though they can increase the amount of surplus value extracted. This seems obviously wrong. Future capitalists will not find their profits drying up as they replace their last workers by intelligent robots. Instead, the profits will flow from their competitive advantage over other manufacturers who produce at higher cost because they are still paying human workers. Alternatively, if other manufacturers also turn to robots, profits will still be earned by those capitalists who are best in designing or marketing the products the robots will make.

Many of Marx's other theories have been refuted by events: the theory that wages will always tend downwards to the subsistence level of the workers; the theory of the falling rate of profit; the theory that under capitalism economic crises will become more and more severe; the theory that capitalism will force more and more people down into the working class; and the theory that, to force wages down, capitalism requires an 'industrial reserve army' of paupers, people who are unemployed or irregularly employed, and living near the subsistence level.

Does this mean that the central theses of *Capital* are simply mistaken, and that the work is just another piece of crackpot economics—as we might have expected from a German philosopher meddling in a field in which he has not been trained? If this view seems at all plausible, Marx himself, with his emphasis on the scientific nature of his discovery, must bear the blame. It would be better to regard *Capital*, not as the work of 'a minor post-Ricardian' (as Paul Samuelson, a leading 20th-century economist, once appraised Marx as an economist), but as the work of a critic of capitalist society. Marx wanted to expose the deficiencies of classical economics in order to expose the deficiencies of capitalism. He wanted to show why the enormous increase in productivity and wealth brought about by the industrial revolution had made the great majority of human beings worse off than before. He wanted to reveal how the old relationships of master and slave, lord and serf, survived under the cloak of freedom of contract. His answer to these questions was the doctrine of surplus value. As an economic doctrine it does not stand up to scientific probing. Marx's economic theories are not a scientific account of the nature and extent of exploitation under capitalism. They nevertheless offer a vivid picture of the kind of society created by the forces unleashed by capitalism: a society in which the productive workers unconsciously create the instruments of their own oppression. It is a picture of human alienation, writ large as the dominance of past labour, or capital, over living labour. The value of the picture lies in its capacity to lead us to see its subject in a radically new way. It is a work of art, of philosophical reflection, and of social polemic, all in one, and it has the merits and the defects of all three of these forms of writing. It is a painting of capitalism, not a photograph.

Chapter 9
Communism and revolution

How communism would be achieved

In his speech at Marx's funeral, Engels said that although the materialist conception of history and the doctrine of surplus value were Marx's crowning theoretical discoveries:

> Marx was before all else a revolutionist. His real mission in life was to contribute, in one way or another, to the overthrow of capitalist society and of the state institutions which it had brought into being, to contribute to the liberation of the modern proletariat...

To complete our account of Marx's main ideas, therefore, we need to ask two questions. How, in Marx's view, would capitalism be overthrown? And what kind of society did Marx believe would take the place of capitalism?

Describing Marx as 'a revolutionist' indicates that Marx believed a revolution would be required to overthrow capitalism. That is the clear message of *The Communist Manifesto:*

> In depicting the most general phases of the development of the proletariat, we traced the more or less veiled civil war, raging within existing society, up to the point where that war breaks out into open revolution, and where the violent overthrow of the bourgeoisie lays the foundation for the sway of the proletariat.   (*CM* 254)

Later, however, Marx did not rule out the possibility of a democratic transition. According to newspaper reports of remarks he made during a visit to Holland in 1872, he acknowledged that in some countries—he mentioned America, England, and possibly Holland itself—workers might be able to obtain their goal by peaceful means. Engels also described Marx as having thought that in England the revolution might be both 'peaceful and legal'. (See Figure 9.)

In the 20th century, communist parties in several European democracies often refused to cooperate with Social Democrats in order to gain power peacefully. Their view was that social democratic reforms like the introduction of a welfare state would make capitalism more tolerable and so serve to postpone the revolution that would bring about communism. This was especially tragic in Germany, where at the last free election before Hitler was appointed Chancellor, the Social Democrats and Communists together won more seats than the Nazis and could

9. The Paris Commune of 1871, which Marx described in *The Civil War in France*, and is often regarded as the first communist revolution.

have kept Hitler out of power if they had been willing to work together. It is therefore worth noting that Marx was not opposed to attempts to get better conditions for workers, even when they fell far short of communism, but better conditions were not his real goal. In *The Communist Manifesto* Marx and Engels refer to the successful battle for legislation limiting the working day to ten hours, and say that the 'real fruit' of such struggles is that they help to form the workers into a class and a political party (*CM* 252).

Marx's reluctance to describe communism

What would be the outcome of the revolution that Marx was expecting? The easy answer is: communism. The difficult task is to say what Marx meant by communism.

There is a reason for Marx's reticence over the details of communist society. He believed that history owed its momentum to the development of the forces of production rather than the development of ideas. This does not mean that theory is unimportant. If Marx's mission in life was to contribute to the overthrow of capitalism and the liberation of the proletariat, his theories of history and of economics were intended to do this by showing the workers their role in history and making them conscious of the manner in which capitalism exploited them. While theory could describe existing reality in this way, however, for theory to reach ahead of its time was another matter altogether. Marx derided as 'utopian' those socialists who thought that the way to bring about communism is to produce a blueprint of a future communist society in which everyone works happily together and no one has to live in poverty. In contrast to these utopian socialists, Marx claimed that his work had a scientific basis because it was built on knowledge of the laws of history that would bring socialism into existence.

Along with his rejection of utopian views of socialism, and for the same reason, Marx condemned conspiratorial revolutionaries who wished to capture power and introduce socialism before the economic base of society had developed to the point at which the working class as a whole was ready to participate in the revolution. Utopian dreamers and revolutionary conspirators fancy that the laws of history will bend to their desires. Marx prided himself on his freedom from this delusion. He saw his role as raising the revolutionary consciousness of the workers and preparing for the revolution that would occur when conditions were ripe. He thought he could describe the underlying laws governing the past and his own time, but he knew he could not impose his own will on the course of history. Nor could he predict the form to be taken by the new society that would be built by the free human beings of the new era.

What Marx did say about communism

That, at least, was Marx's official position. In practice he could not refrain entirely from hinting at the form communist society might take.

We have seen that in his first discussion, in the *Economic and Philosophic Manuscripts of 1844*, Marx described communism as 'the riddle of history solved' and as the resolution of various conflicts that have existed throughout all previous history: the conflicts between man and nature, between man and man, between freedom and necessity, and between individual and species. This conception of communism is thoroughly utopian, in the common sense of the word, rather than in the specific sense Marx was later to use. In 1844 Marx saw communism as the answer to every problem, and indeed as a virtual paradise on earth.

A similarly utopian conception of communism can be found in *The German Ideology*, where Marx suggests that in communist society the division of labour would not force us into narrow occupational roles. I could, Marx says, 'hunt in the morning, fish in the afternoon, breed cattle in the evening, criticize after dinner, just as I have a mind, without ever becoming hunter, fisherman, cowherd, or critic' (*GI* 185). More important than this idyllic image of pastoral communism, however, is Marx's claim in the same passage that the split between the particular interests of the individual and the common interest of society would disappear under communism. This is in line with his earlier remarks about communism resolving such conflicts as that between man and man, and between the individual and the species. It is crucial to Marx's vision of communism. Marx immediately goes on to say that it is out of this very contradiction between the interest of the individual and the community that the state develops as an independent entity. So an understanding of how this contradiction can be overcome should enable us to understand the famous Marxist doctrine that under communism the state will be superseded.

In proposing a solution to the problem of the individual and the community, Marx was contributing to a tradition in moral philosophy going back at least to Plato. Plato had argued that personal happiness is to be found in virtuous conduct and in serving one's community. He thus found harmony between the individual's interest in happiness and the needs of the community. But Plato's arguments did not convince later philosophers.

Marx thought the division between individual interest and community interest was a feature of a particular stage of human development, rather than an inevitable aspect of social existence, a feature which had existed ever since the break-up of very simple societies in which people had lived communally, without private ownership and division of labour. Capitalism, however, heightened the conflict by turning everything into a commodity, leaving 'no other nexus between man and man than naked self-interest, than callous "cash payment"' (*CM* 247).

How did Marx think the opposition between private and communal interests could be overcome? Obviously the abolition of private property could play a part—it is not so easy to feather one's own nest if one doesn't own any feathers, or a nest. But the change would have to go deeper, for even without private property people could pursue their own interests by trying to get as much as they could for themselves (for immediate consumption if the abolition of private property made hoarding impossible) or by shirking their share of the work necessary to keep the community going, especially when the work is arduous or dangerous. To alter this, nothing short of a radical transformation of human nature would suffice.

Here the materialist conception of history underpins the possibility of communism. According to Marx's view of history, as the economic basis of society is transformed, so is our consciousness. Greed, egoism, and envy are not ingrained forever in the character of human beings. They would disappear in a society in which private property and private means of production were replaced with communal property and socially organized means of production. We would lose our preoccupation with our private interests. Citizens of the new society would find their own happiness in working for the good of all. Hence a communist society would have a new ethical basis.

Marx's ethics

It has been claimed—by Lenin among others—that Marxism is a scientific system, free from any ethical judgements or postulates. This cannot be correct. Marx did not just predict that capitalism would be overthrown and replaced by communism; he judged the change to be desirable. He did not need to make this judgement explicit, as it was implied by everything he wrote about capitalism and communism, and by his unceasing political activity. Marx's ethical attitudes are woven into his conception of human progress through alienation to the final state of complete freedom.

The belief that Marxism contains no ethical judgements derives from some comments made by Marx and Engels. In *The Communist Manifesto*, for instance, morality is listed together with law and religion as 'bourgeois prejudices, behind which lurk in ambush just as many bourgeois interests' (*CM* 254). That follows from the materialist conception of history, which regards morality as part of the ideological superstructure of society. Hence the particular morality of any society is determined by the economic basis, and serves to promote the interests of the ruling class. That view may lead Marxists to reject morality as serving the interests of the ruling class, and Marxists will consider that this has been true of all dominant moralities up to now. Once communism has been established and classes have disappeared, however, we will pass beyond class morality, to what Engels called 'a really human morality'.

As with communism in general, so with communist morality one can only guess at its detailed content. Communism would differ from all previous societies in that there would be no false consciousness. False consciousness involves failing to see things as they really are. It comes about because a society's superstructure can conceal the real basis of the society. So, for example, the legal freedom of the worker to sell his labour to whomever he likes on whatever terms he likes conceals the fact that he is really no more able to avoid exploitation by capitalists than the feudal serf is free to avoid working on his lord's land. Class morality adds an extra layer of false consciousness, leading the worker to believe that, for example, the capitalist has a moral right to the proceeds of his investment.

In a communist system of production there would be no exploitation to be concealed. Everything would really be as it appeared to be. Moral illusions would crumble along with the religious illusions against which the Young Hegelians so fiercely argued. The new human morality would not hypocritically cloak sectional interests in a universal guise. It would be genuinely universal, because it would serve the interests of all human beings.

The new communist morality would have a character quite different from previous moralities, and different even from moralities like utilitarianism that proclaim their equal concern for all. Though Marx was as scornful of utilitarianism as of any other ethical theory, his scorn was directed at the utilitarian conception of the general interest rather than at the basic utilitarian idea of maximizing happiness—in fact Marx refers to this idea as 'a homespun...commonplace', which does not imply that he disagrees with it (*C* I 758). But in capitalist society, to propose that people act for the general interest is often to propose that they work against their own interest, as they conceive it. Under such conditions the very idea of morality implies something burdensome and contrary to our own interests. Under communism this aspect of morality will vanish as the gulf between individual interest and universal interest vanishes. Morality will cease to be a dictate from without and become an expression of our chief wants as social beings.

It has been said that later in life Marx developed a less utopian view of communism, but it is difficult to find much evidence of this. There is one passage in the third volume of *Capital* in which Marx, in sharp contrast to his earlier vision of communism in the *Economic and Philosophic Manuscripts*, sees the conflict between freedom and necessity as ineliminable. This is the passage, already cited, in which Marx says that freedom begins 'only where labour determined by necessity and external expediency ends'. He goes on to say that it is part of the 'very nature' of things that when we are producing to satisfy our needs we are not free. Shortening the working day is, therefore, the prerequisite of freedom (*C* III 959). This implies that the conflict between freedom and necessity cannot be entirely overcome, and the best we will be able to achieve is to reduce the amount of necessary labour to a minimum, thereby increasing the time that we are free. That thought contrasts oddly with what Marx says about communism in his comments on the Gotha Programme—also a late work—which are as optimistic as any of his early statements. There Marx foresees the end of the 'enslaving subordination of the individual to the division of labour' and looks forward to a time when labour will become 'not only a means of life, but life's prime want' (GP 615).

The idea of labour as 'life's prime want' seems very different from the clock-watching attitude that takes the shortening of the working day as the prerequisite of freedom. Can these two views be reconciled? Perhaps, if we stress that in the first passage, Marx was treating as a limit to our freedom, only labour that is determined by 'necessity and external expediency'. Perhaps it will eventually be possible to replace that kind of labour by artificially intelligent machines. If this happened in a communist society, the production of these machines would be distributed to everyone—for example by the payment of a universal basic income—and people could choose to engage in more creative labour in which they value what they are producing for its own sake, and not merely because it provides them with the means to buy the necessities of life.

In these comments on the Gotha Programme Marx proposes the celebrated principle of distribution for a communist society: 'from each according to his ability, to each according to his needs'. The principle is not original to Marx, and Marx places little emphasis upon it. He refers to it only in order to criticize those socialists who worry too much about how goods would be distributed in a socialist society. Marx thought it a mistake to bother about working out a fair principle of distribution. He describes such ideas as 'obsolete verbal rubbish' and was willing to allow that, given the capitalist mode of production, capitalist distribution was the only one that was 'fair' because 'right can never be higher than the economic structure of society'. Marx's aim in this section of his critique is to show that it is 'a crime' to force on the Party dogmas like 'fair distribution' and 'equal right' because it would pervert the more realistic outlook he favoured. Production, not distribution, is what matters, for once the means of production are owned cooperatively by the workers, and 'the productive forces have increased with the all-round development of the individual, and all the springs of cooperative wealth flow more abundantly', distribution will look after itself (GP 615).

Communist abundance and the withering away of the state

Everything Marx says about communism is premised on material abundance. Remember that the driving force behind historical change is, according to the materialist theory of history, the development of the forces of production. The change from one form of society to another occurs when the existing structure of society acts as a fetter on the further development of the productive forces. But communism is the final form of society. Communism will therefore inherit the dramatic advances in production so ruthlessly made by capitalism, and will allow these forces to develop to their fullest possible extent. Production will be cooperatively planned for the benefit of all, not wasted in socially fruitless competition between individual capitalists for their own private ends. There will be no crises of overproduction, as there are in unplanned economies. The reserve army of unemployed workers required by capitalism to keep labour cheap and available will be employed and become productive. Mechanization and automation will continue to develop as they had developed under capitalism, though without their degrading effect on the workers, and presumably with a drastic reduction in the hours of necessary labour. No longer will surplus value be extracted from the workers to line the pockets of the capitalists. The working class will receive the full use-value of its labour, subject only to a deduction for future social investment. We will control our economy, instead of being controlled by it.

Material abundance and the transformation of human nature provide the basis for Marx's claim that the state as we know it would cease to exist under communism. This would not happen immediately, for at first the proletariat would have to assert itself over the other classes, in order to abolish capitalist forms of production. This would be the 'dictatorship of the proletariat' (GP 611). But once capitalist production had been replaced by socialist production the division of society into classes would disappear, along with conflicts between individual and social interests. There would be no need for political power in the Marxist sense of the organized power of one class used to oppress another. Nor, given Marx's idea that communism would come first to the most industrially advanced societies, and would be international in character, would there be any need for the state in the sense of an organization existing to defend the nation against attacks from other nations. Relieved from oppressive conditions that bring their interests into conflict, people would voluntarily cooperate with each other. The political state resting on armed force would, in Engels's words, 'wither away'. Its place would be taken by 'an association, in which the free development of each is the condition for the free development of all' (*CM* 262).

Chapter 10
Was Marx right?

An assessment

Any exposition of Marx's ideas is also an assessment of them. In arguing that Marx's main achievements—his theory of history and his economics—are not scientific discoveries, I have already rejected the accolade bestowed on Marx by Engels, confirmed by Lenin, and echoed by orthodox Marxist-Leninists ever since. If Marx did not make scientific discoveries about economics and society, however, what did he get right? (See Figure 10.)

First, though, it is necessary to say a little more about Marx as a scientist; for it cannot be denied that Marx thought of his own theories as 'scientific', and based predictions about the future of capitalism on them. He predicted that:

> While capitalists get richer, workers' wages will, with a few short-lived exceptions, remain at or near the subsistence level.
> More and more independent producers will be forced down into the proletariat, leaving a few rich capitalists and a growing mass of poor workers.
> The rate of profit will fall.
> Capitalism will collapse or be overthrown because of its internal contradictions.

10. Karl Marx.

Proletarian revolutions will occur in the most industrially advanced
countries.

More than a century after Marx made these predictions, most of
them are so plainly mistaken that one can only wonder why
anyone sympathetic to Marx would attempt to argue that his
greatness lies in the scientific aspects of his work. In industrialized
countries, workers' real wages have risen far above bare subsistence.
Rates of profit rise and fall in different times and places, but the
long-term decline that Marx predicted has not eventuated.
Capitalism has gone through several crises, but nowhere has it
collapsed or been overthrown as a result of internal contradictions.
Communists have taken power in less developed nations, rather
than in the more industrialized ones.

scientists test their theories by drawing predictions from them, and then checking whether the predictions are accurate. A scientific theory that yielded predictions as far astray as Marx's predictions would have to be abandoned, or at a minimum, heavily revised. It is better to think of Marx as a philosopher—in the broadest sense—than as a scientist. His predictions were derived from his application of Hegel's philosophy to the progress of human history and the economics of capitalism. Hegel, like Marx, described his work as 'scientific'. The German term they both used (*Wissenschaft*) includes any serious, systematic study, and in that sense, of course, Marx and Hegel were both scientists; but the modern sense of the English word is narrower, and it is in this narrower sense that Engels and Marxists who came after him claimed that Marx made scientific discoveries. We regard Hegel as a philosopher, not a scientist, and we should think of Marx primarily in the same way.

As a philosopher, Marx's work endures. It has altered our understanding of our history and our social existence, and deepened our grasp of what it is to be free.

Freedom was Marx's central concern—paradoxical as this may seem when we look at the regimes that have professed to follow his ideas. The significance of Marx's idea of freedom is best appreciated by contrasting it with the standard liberal notion of freedom accepted—in Marx's time and in our own—by opponents of government interference with the free market. According to this liberal view, I am free so long as I am not subject to deliberate interference from other people. My own freedom can rightly be restricted only to ensure greater freedom for all, so freedom is at its maximum when each individual is able to act without deliberate interference from others.

This conception of freedom fits perfectly with the economic theories of defenders of unrestrained capitalism, for they portray capitalism as the outcome of the free choices of millions of individuals. The capitalist offers people work at, say, £8 an hour, for forty hours a week. Anyone can choose, without interference from others, to accept or reject this offer. If some accept it, the capitalist uses their labour, say, to make shirts. She offers these shirts for sale at a certain price, and again anyone can freely choose whether to buy them at this price. Those who think they can make shirts better or more cheaply than the capitalists now in business are free to set up their own enterprises.

The way capitalism really works isn't quite so simple, but this outline shows how the liberal view of freedom can be used to provide a defence of capitalism that is immune to the objection that capitalists are greedy people who exploit the poor by selling at exorbitant prices. Defenders of capitalism can readily admit that some capitalists may be greedy, but they can also point out that no one is forced to work for or buy from any individual capitalist. So the greed of individual capitalists is not a reason for condemning the free enterprise system.

Marx saw that within its own terms this defence of capitalism is coherent; but he also saw that from a broader, historical perspective, the liberal definition of freedom is open to a fundamental objection. An everyday example illustrates this objection. Suppose I live in the suburbs and work in the city. I could drive my car to work, or take the bus. I prefer not to wait for the bus, so I take my car. Fifty thousand other people living in my suburb make the same decision. The road to town is choked with cars. It takes each of us an hour to travel ten kilometres.

We have all chosen freely, for no one deliberately interfered with our choices; yet the outcome is something none of us wants. If we all went by bus, the roads would be empty and we could be at work in twenty minutes. Even with the inconvenience of waiting at the bus stop, we would all prefer that. We are, of course, free to take the bus, but all the other cars on the road slow the bus down, so none of us has a sufficient reason to do so. We have each chosen in our own interests, but the result is in no one's interests. Individual rationality, collective irrationality.

The solution, obviously, is for us all to get together and make a collective decision. Together we can achieve what we want, subject only to the physical limits of our resources and technology. In this example, we can all agree to use the bus, or at least to create bus lanes so the bus can move rapidly even when traffic is heavy.

Marx recognized that in pre-capitalist systems it was obvious that most people did not control their own destiny. Under feudalism, for instance, serfs had to work for their lords. Capitalism seems different because people are in theory free to work for themselves or for others as they choose. Yet Marx saw that most workers have as little control over their lives as feudal serfs. This is not because they have chosen badly. Nor is it because of the physical limits of our resources and technology. It is because the cumulative effect of countless individual choices is a society that no one—not even the capitalists—has chosen. Where those who hold the liberal conception of freedom would say we are free because we are not subject to deliberate interference by other humans, Marx says we are not free because we do not control the social and economic arrangements that dominate our lives. Economic relations between human beings determine not only our wages and our prospects of finding work, but also our politics, our religion, and our ideas. These economic relations force us into a situation in which we compete with each other instead of cooperating for the good of all. That nullifies the technical advances we have made in the use of our resources. Rationally organized, industrialization should enable us to enjoy an abundance of material goods with a minimum of effort. Under capitalism, however, these advances simply reduce the value of the commodity produced, which means that the worker must work just as long for the same wage. Worse still, the absence of any overall planning or direction in the economy leads to crises of overproduction—in itself a clear indication of an irrational system—and to recessions in which the economy operates in a manner that neither workers nor capitalists desire. (Here Marx's point retains some truth, as governments still struggle to provide full employment and avoid recession while restraining inflation.)

Economic relations appear to us as blind natural forces. We do not see them as restricting our freedom—and indeed on the liberal conception of freedom they do not restrict our freedom, since they are not the result of deliberate human interference. Marx himself is quite explicit that the capitalist is not individually responsible for the economic relations of his society, but is controlled by these relations as much as the workers are (*C* I 92). Yet these economic relations are our own unwitting creations, not deliberately chosen but nevertheless the outcome of our own individual choices and thus potentially subject to our will. We are not truly free until, instead of letting our creations control us, we collectively take control of them. That is why Marx favours moving to a planned economy. In an unplanned economy, human beings unwittingly grant the market control over their lives. If we all plan the economy cooperatively we will, in Marx's view, be reasserting our freedom as a community or even as a species.

Marx's penetrating critique of liberal political philosophy lies at the core of his attack on alienation in the 1844 *Manuscripts*, and is a key element in his analysis of capitalism. Its roots derive from Hegel, whose historical perspective enabled him to see that our wants and needs are shaped by the society in which we live. Although today's consumer society still lay far ahead, Hegel grasped that in a free market society, our desire for greater comfort is not innate, but suggested to us by those who seek to profit from it. Marx went further, seeing how capitalism, like other modes of production, shapes not only our desires and thus our human nature, but also our ideas and our institutions. If Marx has any claim to a place alongside Hobbes, Locke, Rousseau, and Hegel as a major political philosopher, it rests on his critique of the liberal conception of freedom.

The alternative conception of freedom Marx espoused does, however, face a difficulty: how do we obtain the cooperation of each individual in the joint endeavour of controlling our economy and our society? This unsolved—and largely unaddressed—problem in Marx's critique of liberal freedom is one of the threads that link his theory with the murderously authoritarian regimes that subsequently purported to follow his ideas. Return for a moment to our example of the commuters. They hold a meeting. All agree that it would be better to leave their cars at home. They part, rejoicing at the prospect of no more traffic jams. But in the privacy of their own homes, some reason to themselves: 'If everyone else is going to take the bus tomorrow, the roads will be empty. So I'll take my car. Then I'll have the convenience of door-to-door transportation *and* the advantage of a traffic-free run.' From a self-interested point of view this reasoning is sound. As long as most take the bus, a few others can free ride on the socially minded behaviour of the majority, without giving up anything themselves.

What should the majority do? Should they leave it up to the conscience of each individual to decide whether to play their part? If they do, there is a risk that the system will break down—once a few take their own cars, others will soon follow, for no one likes to be taken advantage of. Or should the majority attempt to coerce the minority into taking the bus? That can be done in the name of freedom for all, and it may be the right thing to do, but it risks leading to freedom for none—especially if the bus company has a monopoly and becomes inefficient.

Marx was devoted to the cause of human freedom. When asked, in a Victorian parlour game, to name the vice he most detested, he replied: 'Servility'; and as his favourite motto he put down: 'De omnibus dubitandum'—'You must have doubts about everything' (MC 430). Though his own personality had an authoritarian streak, there can be little doubt he would have been appalled at the power Lenin and Stalin wielded in his name, and if, miraculously, he had been alive and living in Russia in the 1930s, he would surely have been a victim of Stalin's purges.

Here Marx's second major contribution to philosophical thinking—his view of human nature—ties in with his idea of freedom. Marx's insight that human nature is not fixed, but alters in accordance with the economic and social conditions of each period, holds out the prospect of transforming society by changing the economic basis of such human traits as greed, egoism, and ambition. Marx expected the abolition of private property and the institution of common ownership of the means of production and exchange to bring about a society in which people were motivated more by a desire for the good of all than by a specific desire for their own individual good. In this way individual and common interests could be harmonized. Coercion would be unnecessary because communism would end the conflict between individual interests and the common good. The state, as an agent of coercion, could then wither away, leaving only administrative functions to be run by the workers.

Important elements of Marx's view of human nature are now so widely accepted that a return to a pre-Marxist conception of human nature is unthinkable. Though Marx's own theory is not scientific, it laid the foundations for a new social science that would explore the relations between such apparently unconnected areas of life as the tools people use to produce food and their political and religious beliefs. This has been a fruitful area for historians and social scientists to investigate. In opening it up, Marx shattered the assumption that our intellectual and spiritual lives develop independently of our economic existence. If 'Know thyself' is the first imperative of philosophy, Marx's contribution to our self-understanding is another reason for ranking him highly among philosophers.

Once Marx has been given due credit for making us aware of the economic and social forces that may influence us, however, it has to be added that he took his insights to an extreme that led him to false and even naive views. Human nature is not as pliable as Marx believed. Egoism, for instance, is not eliminated by economic reorganization nor by material abundance. When basic needs are satisfied, new 'needs' emerge. In our society, people want not simply clothes, but fashionable clothes; not merely shelter from the weather, but a house to display their wealth and taste. Granted, capitalist enterprises spend billions of dollars trying to persuade us that we need things that we really do not need, but we cannot put all the blame on advertising. Desires to own and consume items that are not necessary for our physical health and well-being emerge in the non-capitalist world as well, often in the face of disapproval from the official ideology. Unless rigid uniformity is imposed—and perhaps even then—these desires will find an outlet. Nor will it ever be possible to satisfy everyone's material desires. How could we provide everyone with a house in a secluded position overlooking the sea, but within easy reach of the city?

In different societies, egoistic desires take different forms. This does not show that they can be abolished altogether, but only that they are the expression of a more basic desire. There is, for instance, more than simple greed behind our insatiable urge for consumer goods. There is also the desire for status, and perhaps sometimes a desire for the power that status can bring. No doubt capitalism accentuates these desires. There are societies in which competition for status and power are restrained, when compared to, say, the United States in the 21st century. There may even be societies lacking any such competition. Yet desires for status and power exist in many human beings, in a range of different societies. They tend to surface despite sustained efforts to suppress them. No society, no matter how egalitarian its rhetoric, has succeeded in abolishing the distinction between ruler and ruled. Nor has any society succeeded in making this distinction *merely* a matter of who leads and who follows: to be a ruler gives one special status and, usually, special privileges. During the era of

Soviet communism, important officials in the Soviet Union had access to special shops selling delicacies unavailable to ordinary citizens. Before China allowed capitalist enterprises in its economy, travelling by car was a luxury limited to tourists and those high in the party hierarchy (and their families). Throughout the 'communist' nations, the abolition of the old ruling class was followed by the rise of a new class of party bosses and well-placed bureaucrats, whose behaviour and lifestyle came more and more to resemble that of their much-denounced predecessors. (George Orwell brilliantly satirized this process in the changing lifestyle of the ruling pigs in *Animal Farm*.) In the end, hardly anyone believed in the Soviet form of communism.

What is to be learnt from these attempts to create communist societies? Early in his career, Marx formulated his view of human nature in one of his 'Theses on Feuerbach': '...the human essence is no abstraction inherent in each single individual. In its reality it is the ensemble of the social relations' (T 172). That statement involves an important insight—human nature is affected by the prevailing social relations, and so is different in different kinds of society—but it is misleadingly one-sided. There *are* elements of human nature that are inherent in most (if not all) human individuals. Changing the social relations, or the economic basis of society, will not eliminate them. Marx's mistake about human nature helps to explain the failures of several forms of communism that have claimed to be Marxist. On the question of whether and to what extent changing social and economic conditions will change human nature, we now have a great deal of relevant evidence that was not available to Marx. This includes evidence of the failure of deliberate attempts to create egalitarian societies on the basis of the abolition of private ownership of the means of production, and evidence of the hierarchical nature of human societies, whether capitalist or not, and of non-human societies as well, including social mammals. There are evolutionary reasons why this should be so. Among social mammals, higher-ranking individuals have advantages in reproducing and in ensuring the survival of their offspring. In these species, the tendency to compete for status is therefore likely to have been selected for during millions of years of evolution, and now to be innate. Humans are social mammals, and it would be surprising if we, or many of us, had not also inherited a desire to rise up hierarchies, whether of power, or wealth, or social status. If we have, it will not be nearly as easy as Marx thought to bring the conflicting interests of human beings into harmony.

This conclusion has far-reaching consequences for Marx's positive proposals. If changing the economic basis of society will not bring individuals to see their own interests and the interests of society as the same, then communism as Marx conceived it must be abandoned. Marx never intended a communist society to force the individual to work against his or her own interests for the collective good—at least not for longer than the brief period in which the economic structure of the society was in the process of transitioning to social ownership, and human nature was adjusting to this change, as Marx assumed it would. The need to use coercion would signify not the overcoming of alienation, but the continuing alienation of man from man; a coercive society would not be the riddle of history solved, but merely the riddle restated in a new form; it would not end class rule, but would substitute a new ruling class for the old one. We should not blame Marx for dictatorships that he did not foresee and which, if he had foreseen them, he would have condemned. Nevertheless, the distance between the communist society Marx envisaged and the form taken by 'communism' in the 20th century may in the end be traceable to his mistaken conception of the plasticity of human nature.

It is both sad and ironic to read today some marginal jottings Marx made in 1874, while reading Bakunin's *Statism and Anarchy*. Marx copied out passages from this work by his anarchist rival from the days of the First International, and then made his own comments on each passage. Thus the jottings read like a dialogue, one section of which goes like this:

BAKUNIN: Universal suffrage by the whole people of representatives and rulers of the state—this is the last word of the Marxists as well as of the democratic school. They are lies behind which lurks the despotism of a governing minority, lies all the more dangerous in that this minority appears as the expression of the so-called people's will.

MARX: Under collective property, the so-called will of the people disappears in order to make way for the real will of the co-operative.

BAKUNIN: Result: rule of the great majority of the people by a privileged minority. But, the Marxists say, this minority will consist of workers. Yes, indeed, but of ex-workers who, once they become only representatives or rulers of the people, cease to be workers.

MARX: No more than a manufacturer today ceases to be a capitalist when he becomes a member of the municipal council.

BAKUNIN: And from the heights of the State they begin to look down upon the whole common world of the workers. From that time on they represent not the people but themselves and their own claims to govern the people. Those who can doubt this know nothing at all about human nature.

MARX: If Mr Bakunin were in the know, if only with the position of a manager in a workers' co-operative, he would send all his nightmares about authority to the devil. He should have asked himself: what form can administrative functions assume on the basis of that workers' state, if it pleases him to call it thus? (B 608)

The tragedy of Marxism is that our experience of the rule of workers in several different countries bears out Bakunin's objections, rather than Marx's replies. In figures like Joseph Stalin, Mao Zedong, Kim Il Sung, and Pol Pot, Bakunin's 'nightmares about authority' came horribly true.

There is one other element of Marx's views that, with the benefit of hindsight, we may consider conducive to authoritarian forms of communism. One of Marx's predictions, as we have seen, was that the proletarian revolutions that abolished private property would occur in the most advanced industrialized countries, in which the working class constituted the overwhelming majority of the population. Since the workers owned nothing, and were living close to subsistence, they had, as Marx and Engels famously pointed out, 'nothing to lose but their chains' (*CM* 271). They could, therefore, reasonably be expected to be enthusiastic supporters of communism. In fact, however, the first successful communist revolution took place in Russia, the least industrialized of the major European powers. In 1917, Russia's small industrialized working class was heavily outnumbered by agricultural workers and small rural landholders. Rural areas are typically more conservative than urban areas, and rural landholders stood to lose a great deal from the abolition of private property. It is not surprising, therefore, that communism could only be imposed on Russia with the use of considerable force and, when resistance appeared, increasing brutality that led to the murder and incarceration of millions of people.

Subsequent communist revolutions were also successful in countries with little or no industrialization (at least if we set aside those countries in which communists achieved power because of Soviet influence): for example, in China, North Korea, Vietnam, Cuba, Cambodia, and Laos. In all of these countries the communist governments took authoritarian forms, though with varying degrees of oppression.

Marx saw that capitalism is a wasteful, irrational system that controls us when we should be controlling it. That insight is still valid; but we can now see that the construction of a free and equal society is a far more difficult task than Marx realized.

Chapter 11
Is Marx still relevant?

Marx's prominence

As the decades passed after Marx's death, his work received increasing recognition. By the early 20th century, Marxism was the dominant ideology of the left, especially in Europe. Marx's influence grew as socialist parties gained popularity, especially in Germany, where before the First World War, the Social Democratic Party received more votes than any other political party. The success of the Bolshevik revolution in Russia in 1917 increased Marx's prominence still further. From the end of the First World War, in 1918, to the end of the Second World War, the great ideological battles were between Marxism, fascism, and liberal democracy. After 1945 the Red Army brought the Soviet version of Marxism to much of Eastern and Central Europe. China became Marxist, as did North Korea, North Vietnam, Cuba, and eventually a unified Vietnam, as well as Cambodia and Laos. Meanwhile Marxist political parties or revolutionary movements increased their influence in Africa, Latin America, and the Indian subcontinent. The forty-year period after 1945 was the high tide of Marx's reputation, as measured by the extent to which regimes celebrated his work. Whether we also regard it as the high tide of Marx's influence depends on the extent to which we judge that the communist regimes properly reflected Marx's ideas, or were a grotesque distortion of them.

Marx's prominence went into abrupt decline in 1991, when the Soviet Union collapsed and its constituent parts, as well as its former European satellites, abandoned communism. From that time on, by far the most significant country to embrace Marxism has been China. Any discussion of Marx's relevance in the world today must start with the fact that almost 1.4 billion Chinese live under the rule of the Communist Party of China, which according to its constitution adheres to Marxism-Leninism, as well as views developed by Mao Zedong, Deng Xiaoping, and more recent Chinese leaders. Officially, Marx's ideas are regarded as the basis for all of these views, and the outcome is described as 'socialism with Chinese characteristics'. (See Figure 11.)

It is sometimes assumed that the era of reform instituted by Deng Xiaoping in 1978, which allowed private businesses to be established, represented a decisive break with Marxism. Deng famously said that it doesn't matter if a cat is black or white, as long as it catches mice—a remark generally understood to mean that it doesn't matter if enterprises are owned by the state or by individuals, as long as they are efficient in producing what is needed. That does sound like a statement that goes very much against Marx's views. Does this mean that later references to Marxism by China's leaders are mere lip-service?

Deng's economic reforms have been extraordinarily successful, pulling more than 800 million people out of extreme poverty. Today China looks and feels very much like a capitalist country, with a vigorous market economy. The Shanghai stock exchange ranks among the top three in the world, in terms of market capitalization, and China has more billionaires (reckoned in US dollars) than the United States. China's prosperity has come at the cost of a distribution of income that is far less equal than that of the United Kingdom or indeed any nation in Europe, and less equal even than the income distribution of the United States—something else that seems incompatible with the kind of society Marx envisaged. Nevertheless, at the Communist Party

11. A statue of Marx in Chongqing, China.

of China's 95th anniversary in 2016, President Xi Jinping
re-emphasized Marxism, saying, 'The whole party should remember,
what we are building is socialism with Chinese characteristics,
not some other -ism.' That still leaves unexplained just how Marxism
is understood in China, and what 'socialism with Chinese
characteristics' means.

In Chinese hands, Marxism sometimes seems to be emptied of political content. Consider, for example, an article entitled 'The Great Victory of Marxism in China' by Wang Weiguang. The author is no ordinary academic: in 2012 Wang Weiguang became a member of the Central Committee of the Communist Party of China and in the following year he was made President of the Chinese Academy of Social Sciences. How then does this very senior academic and member of China's political elite understand Marxism? Wang Weiguang writes, 'Being committed to Marxism means, in the last analysis, we must follow the ideological line of emancipating our minds and seeking truth from facts...Seeking truth from facts is the living soul of Marxism and the essence of Sinicized Marxism.'

To have an open mind, and seek truth from facts is doubtless a laudable approach, but it can be embraced by pragmatists of all kinds, right or left, not just Marxists. Wang Weiguang does go on to emphasize 'maintaining close ties with the masses'. That is something Marx would have considered essential in a communist party. If, however, the truth we draw from the facts of China's economic success is that the path to prosperity for the masses leads through a capitalist market economy, we may question whether that is still, in any meaningful sense, Marxism. It would not be far-fetched to say that China's poor record of overcoming poverty under the rigid state control of the economy that prevailed under Mao Zedong, combined with its remarkable post-reform economic growth after Deng's opening of the economy, is itself a convincing refutation of Marxist economics. It is ironic that this refutation came about under the guidance of the Communist Party of China.

Inequality

The global financial crisis of 2007–8 led to widespread criticism of the finance industry, and to attempts to regulate it to prevent a recurrence of the risky loans that led to the crisis. That focused attention on the fortunes being made by a few, and so, indirectly, to the Occupy Wall Street movement, which began in 2011 with protests in New York's financial district. Occupy Wall Street took up issues that are consistent with aspects of Marx's critique of capitalism, such as the political influence of corporations and the fact that most of the economic gains of the past decade had gone to the wealthiest 1 per cent. At the time these protests seemed to show that Marx continues to inspire a movement aiming at the overthrow of capitalism. In the end, however, Occupy Wall Street failed to achieve significant changes. The capitalist system was able to absorb the skulduggery and incompetence of individual capitalists and so the crisis demonstrated, once again, capitalism's resilience.

The concerns about inequality raised by Occupy Wall Street were borne out by the French economist Thomas Piketty's surprise bestseller, *Capital in the Twenty-First Century*. The book's title suggests that Piketty saw himself as writing a text that would do for our era what Marx did for his—that is, produce an overall theory of capitalism from which we can predict its future. Piketty's analysis echoes some of Marx's themes, although Piketty is writing within mainstream classical economics, whereas Marx took the stance of an outsider writing a critique. Piketty draws on historical data to argue that, under capitalism, the rate of return on capital investment normally exceeds the rate of economic growth. As a consequence, those with capital to invest increase their wealth at a faster rate than those with labour to sell, even if workers receive, in the form of higher wages, their share of economic growth. The inherent tendency of capitalism is thus to increase inequality.

Piketty does not claim that increasing inequality is inevitable under capitalism no matter what the circumstances. In the aftermath of the Second World War, there was a movement in the opposite direction. Governments introduced higher taxes on the wealthy and better social security for the poor. This came about because fighting through, and recovering from, the devastation of two world wars and the depression of the 1930s required shared sacrifices and a strong sense of community solidarity. That brought about a high rate of economic growth, which made it both possible and desirable to establish a broad system of social welfare, paid for by higher taxes on the wealthy. This 'Golden Age' of relatively egalitarian capitalism lasted for about thirty years. The economist Simon Kuznets saw it as evidence that as countries become richer, inequality diminishes. In contrast, Piketty sees the post-war period as an aberration and the 'Kuznets curve', along with similar widely accepted economic theories, as ideologically tinged Cold War fairy tales that tell us there is no need for communism, because the market economy is making capitalist societies more prosperous *and* more equal.

By 1975 economic growth in Europe and the United States was slowing, inheritance taxes had been abolished or reduced almost to insignificance, and the trend towards inequality soon resumed. We are, according to Piketty, heading back towards the degree of inequality that prevailed in Marx's time, or even in Jane Austen's, when inheriting wealth or finding a rich spouse was a much better economic strategy than working hard. (Piketty resembles Marx in that he mixes literary references in with his economics. For Marx it was Shakespeare and Goethe; for Piketty it is Austen and Balzac.)

Marx, as we have seen, portrayed the tendency of capitalism to profit while workers get poorer with the image of a forest of uplifted arms demanding work, the forest becoming ever thicker while the arms themselves become ever thinner. Piketty does not foresee consequences as dire as the near-starvation implied by the thinning of arms. He does not even argue that the poor will get poorer, in absolute terms. He thinks that once a capitalist economy achieves a high level of income, per capita economic growth is bound to slow to the level generated by technological progress, which he estimates to be around 1–1.5 per cent. This will be true not only for Europe, the United States, and Japan, but also for China, once it catches up with the other affluent nations. Piketty, like Marx, claims to have discovered a general law of capitalist economies, so the same will presumably hold for any other developing economies, such as India, and for African countries too. If per capita economic growth slows, workers' incomes will similarly rise only slowly, while the incomes of those with capital to invest will rise more rapidly. Hence inequality will increase, although workers will, in absolute terms, be better off.

From the perspective of contemporary thinkers sympathetic to a Marxist approach to economics, Piketty's demonstration of capitalism's inherent inegalitarianism is a welcome antidote to the claims of neoclassical economists that the rich have more because they are more productive or more highly skilled. On Piketty's analysis, owning capital is enough to put one among those whose wealth will grow faster than those who live by selling their labour, no matter how highly skilled that labour may be. Marxists can also draw on Piketty's statistics to refute neoclassical economists who argue that the tendency of capitalism to reduce inequality renders the redistributive measures of social democracies unnecessary and even counterproductive. Piketty advocates a tax on capital as the only workable remedy for the increasing inequality generated by capitalism. The problem is that he doubts that such a tax—which would have to be global to prevent capital flowing out of those countries that tax it—is politically feasible.

This is where neo-Marxists find Piketty's analysis falls short of explaining the capitalist tendency to increase inequality. Although Piketty does refer to the top 1 per cent of income recipients as the 'dominant class' he doesn't say much about how this class exercises its power in order to retain its dominance. In the United States the mechanisms by which the dominant class has undermined the democratic ideals of popular sovereignty and political equality are now clearer than ever. The 2010 Supreme Court ruling in the case of *Citizens United v Federal Electoral Commission* that the constitutional protection of freedom of speech precludes governments from restricting many kinds of political spending has led to a few billionaires dramatically increasing their funding of electoral campaigns, and hence their political power. No wonder that Piketty himself recognizes that his proposal for a global wealth tax is 'utopian'.

Marx would not have been surprised to learn that the judicial system of a capitalist society should so clearly place the right of the rich to use their wealth to exercise political power above the democratic ideal of political equality. Still, we should not exaggerate the common ground between Marx and Piketty. Marx thought that under capitalism any increase in workers' wages above the level of subsistence would be short-lived. Piketty knows that in developed capitalist countries workers' wages are far above subsistence, and he thinks they will continue to rise, albeit slowly. Marx thought that capitalism has internal contradictions that are bound to bring about its revolutionary overthrow. Piketty envisions it continuing indefinitely. Only one of them can be right.

Marx in the age of globalization

In a famous passage in *The Communist Manifesto*, Marx and Engels vividly depict the revolutionary power of capitalism to eliminate whatever stands in its way:

> All fixed, fast-frozen relations, with their train of ancient and venerable prejudices and opinions, are swept away, all new-formed ones become antiquated before they can ossify. All that is solid melts into air, all that is holy is profaned, and man is at last compelled to face with sober senses his real conditions of life, and his relations with his kind.

This power, they point out, is not constrained to one country or continent:

> The need of a constantly expanding market for its products chases the bourgeoisie over the entire surface of the globe. It must nestle everywhere, settle everywhere, establish connexions everywhere...All old-established national industries have been destroyed or are daily being destroyed...In place of the old local and national seclusion and self-sufficiency, we have intercourse in every direction, universal inter-dependence of nations. And as in material, so also in intellectual production. The intellectual creations of individual nations become common property. (*CM* 248–9)

If Marx and Engels could already describe capitalism in those terms, today everything happens on a larger scale and at an even more rapid pace. The lowering of barriers to international trade and the consequent growth of manufacturing in Asia has eliminated entire industries from Europe and North America. Digital technology and the internet threaten other industries and professions. Who now remembers Kodak, once the dominant name in film manufacturing? Who consults a telephone directory or navigates around a city with a printed map? Investigative journalism is struggling because the newspapers that once supported it have lost so much advertising revenue to the internet. Taxi drivers who paid large sums for their cab licences suddenly find their income halved by ride-sharing apps. Retail stores selling goods that can be bought online are under threat. The gig economy, in which millions of people make their living as free-lancers, waiting for a text message to get temporary work ranging from consulting services to delivering food, offers more flexibility in work/life balance, but increases economic insecurity. Even these changes seem likely to be minor compared to what the use of robots and artificial intelligence will bring. As Marx and Engels pointed out, intellectual creations become common property, not in the legal sense, but in the sense that the impact of new technologies reaches every corner of the world, whether the software is owned by Apple, Microsoft, or Google, or is open source.

Our era of globalization is Marx's global capitalism on steroids; but he was mistaken about the consequences. Marx predicted that once free trade prevailed, the naked harshness of the laws of economics would apply to the entire planet, thus uniting the international working class and hastening the coming anti-capitalist revolution. It is true that the reduction of international barriers to trade has exposed a much wider section of the world's people to the economic reach of capitalism, but this has not united the international working class, let alone brought about a revolution capable of overthrowing global capitalism.

Some Marxists claim that Marx failed to foresee that the global expansion of capitalism would enable industrialized countries to stave off the revolution, at least temporarily, because the majority of the workers in those countries benefit from the exploitation of workers in developing countries. The more optimistic of these Marxists claim that eventually the workers of the world will see what is happening and unite against it, thus fulfilling Marx's prediction. On this view, all that Marx got wrong was the time-scale on which the revolution would take place.

How much truth is there in this view? We can start by asking whether the present global economic order really is a form of capitalist exploitation of the global poor. In 2017 Oxfam, the international aid organization, ran a campaign pointing out that the eight richest people in the world own as much as the poorest half of the world's population—that is, as much as 3.6 billion people! Such extreme inequality seems blatantly unfair, but from the inequality alone, we cannot conclude that those eight richest people have made their fortunes in ways that caused the poorer half of the world's people to be worse off. It is possible that the billionaires became rich by inventing products made in factories that provided workers with better jobs than they would otherwise have had. The products themselves may also have made impoverished people better off—for example, mobile phones have provided small farmers in undeveloped rural areas with information that enables them to get better prices for their crops. It is also possible, of course, that those eight billionaires made their money in much more harmful ways. To decide whether the worldwide spread of capitalism has made the poor better or worse off, we need to know more.

There is no doubt that some aspects of the world economic order are skewed to favour the rich. To give just one example, multinational corporations buy oil and minerals from dictators who have seized power by force, never held a free election, and will use the payments they receive to buy more weapons to ensure that they cannot be ousted. How different is this from buying stolen goods? It has disastrous consequences for resource-rich developing countries, because it creates a huge incentive for anyone with a strong enough militia to attempt a coup. Yet it goes almost unchallenged, because it provides cheap resources for rich nations.

So yes, capitalism is unfair, and it can be cruel and heartless as well. Strictly speaking, though, none of this has much to do with Marx's views. As we saw when we discussed Marx's ethics in Chapter 9, Marx scorned the idea of putting references to 'fair distribution' or 'equal right' in the programme of the socialist parties meeting in Gotha, describing such phrases as 'obsolete verbal rubbish'. Instead he wanted socialist parties to help the proletariat unite and prepare for the inevitable day when capitalism would be on the brink of collapse and conditions would be ripe for workers to seize control of the means of production and use them for the good of all. If we apply this to our situation in the 21st century, then Marx would be telling us to stop talking about the unfairness of the global economic order and instead work to unite the international proletariat. There are, however, few signs of the formation of an international proletariat that will be able to overthrow global capitalism.

One reason why there is no united international proletariat is that nationalist thinking has proved far stronger and more persistent than internationalists like Marx imagined it would be. Another may be that Marx was mistaken in his belief that under capitalism, whether at a national or a global level, the proportion of people living in poverty would increase and they would remain at or near subsistence level. We can roughly equate subsistence with the line below which the World Bank classifies people as living in 'extreme poverty'—a condition defined as having insufficient income to meet basic needs, such as food, shelter, and clothing. In 1990 the World Bank estimated that there were 1.95 billion people in that condition. By 2016, its estimate was down to 767 million. That decline becomes even more dramatic when we take into account the increase in the world's population over that period. If the proportion of people living in extreme poverty had remained unchanged, there would be 2.7 billion people in that situation, or almost 2 billion more than there are today. In the same period the working middle class of developing countries, defined as people living on more than $4 per day, has grown from only 18 per cent of the workforce in developing countries to half the workforce of those regions. This decrease in extreme poverty is reflected in improvements in other indicators of well-being. In poor countries life expectancy at birth increased, between 1990 and 2012, by an average of nine years. The proportion of people in the world who suffer from hunger was halved between 1990 and 2015. Marx's prediction that capitalism would push more and more people down to the level of bare subsistence has turned out to be mistaken, not only in industrialized countries, but worldwide. For everyone except the most hardened Marxist ideologue, that should be very good news.

Marx and the environmental crisis

In the 21st century we face an unprecedented moral challenge: climate change. We now know that to avert changes in the climate of our planet that would be disastrous for billions of human beings, we need to work together to reduce greenhouse gas emissions. That the human activities underlying the industrial revolution have the power to affect the climate of our planet was, of course, unknown in Marx's day. Are his ideas nevertheless relevant to contemporary concern about this and other environmental issues? Marxists, some of whom describe themselves as 'ecosocialists', endorse Marx's analysis of capitalism as inherently expansionist, relentlessly turning everything, including nature, into commodities on which a profit can be made. Only the overthrow of capitalism, they maintain, will enable us to escape that ceaseless drive for economic growth, and so preserve our environment and anything else that is of more value than the profits that can be made from its destruction. Greens, who try to avoid the left/right political divide, share the ecosocialists' concerns about capitalism, but do not see Marxism as the solution. They point to Marx's emphasis on producing material goods, and his failure to show any concern for the damage that industrialization was already doing to the air, rivers, forests, and animals. They add that environmental despoliation is not limited to capitalist societies: the Soviet Union and its Eastern European satellites were often worse, in that respect, than capitalist Europe, and anyone who has visited Beijing knows that having a communist government does not ensure clean air. Greens therefore strive for a new ethic that rejects consumerism and values the preservation of our environment. Their path to that goal lies through education, but also through green political parties that can achieve change by becoming large enough to take part in governments.

The problem with the strategy of putting the overthrow of capitalism ahead of combating climate change is that we are not likely to get rid of capitalism anytime soon. Meanwhile we will have passed that critical tipping point at which, climate scientists warn us, feedback loops (like the release of methane from the thawing Siberian permafrost) will mean that, even with zero net human greenhouse gas emissions, catastrophic climate change could be unstoppable.

That does not mean that Marx has nothing to tell us about how to slow climate change and deal with other environmental problems. The logic of climate change parallels that of the traffic problem I used in Chapter 10 to illustrate Marx's critique of the liberal concept of freedom. Individuals may believe that they are better off when they can consume more, but collectively they are bringing about an outcome that no one wants. Current predictions are that droughts, floods, and a rise in sea levels will force hundreds of millions of people to become climate refugees. Capitalism cannot deal with this problem unless corporations are compelled to internalize the costs that their greenhouse gas emissions impose on the rest of the world. Taxes on greenhouse gas emissions can achieve that. A 'cap and trade' scheme that provides for a market in permits to emit greenhouse gases is another, and arguably more efficient, way of achieving the same goal. The difficulty is that for this to happen, governments need to act together so that, in a world with few trade barriers, no country is penalized for taking the first step. The task is immense, but not impossible. To prevent dangerous climate change, we need to bring about changes in the way we produce electricity, the cars we drive, and the foods we eat. It is no wonder that not only fossil fuel producers but also some libertarians and free market advocates would rather deny the evidence of climate change than face the challenge it presents to their economic interests and their philosophies about the role of government. Here Marx's analysis of the power of those who benefit most from the existing means of production is again relevant. Capitalists with financial interests in the coal industry have helped to elect politicians who reject the judgements of the overwhelming majority of scientists, supported by a vast amount of research published in peer-reviewed scientific journals, that human activity is changing the climate of our planet in hazardous ways. If we cannot wait for the overthrow of capitalism to do something about this, can we, while living in a capitalist society, overcome the influence of those with financial interests in fossil fuels and take sufficiently strong measures to prevent disaster? We do not yet know the answer.

'The point is, to change it'—but how?

As we have seen, Marx's tombstone has engraved on it words from his eleventh thesis on Feuerbach emphasizing the importance of changing the world (see Figure 12).

We have also seen, however, that Marx led his followers astray by persuading them that victory over capitalism was coming, and would bring about a better world. That prediction meant that the efforts of millions of Marxists to change the world have been misdirected. Although the international communist movement has collapsed, Marx's utopian vision is still leading many people astray. Despite the welcome reduction in the number of people living in extreme poverty, far too many still lack what they need for a minimally decent life. Effective non-profit organizations are working to enable more people to escape extreme poverty, and to have adequate food, safe water, sanitation, education, and basic health care. Many people do support these organizations, but it is common to hear from those on the left that instead of supporting charities, we should overthrow the global capitalist economic order and replace it with a socialist economic order.

This mindset has two fundamental flaws. First, no one has any idea how to achieve the overthrow of the global economic order. Second, no one can point to a system that has been shown, in practice, to deliver better results than capitalism. Marx himself stressed how productive capitalism is. There are no examples of flourishing communist economies in which, to use Marx's words in his 'Critique of the Gotha Programme', 'the springs of co-operative wealth flow more abundantly' than they do under capitalism. Even small-scale attempts to create egalitarian

12. Marx's grave at Highgate Cemetery in London.

communities, like the Israeli kibbutz movement, have largely abandoned their original ideals. The collective settlements now employ outsiders to do much of the hard labour. The hippie communes of the 1970s, some of which began with the explicit intention of demonstrating an alternative to capitalism and consumerism, have almost all disappeared. With no idea how capitalism might be overthrown, and no successful non-capitalist model with which to replace it, dedicating oneself to overthrowing the global capitalist economic order is like setting out on an arduous and perilous voyage to a destination that one may never reach, and, if one does reach it, may prove to be worse than one's starting point.

In the dark days of the Second World War the Austrian philosopher Karl Popper, then living in New Zealand, argued for 'piecemeal social engineering' rather than 'utopian social engineering'. By 'piecemeal social engineering' he meant small-scale incremental changes, targeted at the greatest and most urgent social evils, and carried out in an open-minded manner by people willing to be guided by the outcomes they observe. In contrast, utopian social engineers attempt to bring about the best possible society, and are too dogmatic about what needs to be done to allow awkward facts to get in the way, which makes failure likely. Moreover, there are always opportunities for piecemeal social engineering, whereas advocates of utopian social schemes need to wait for the right moment, which may never come, all the while passing up promising opportunities for practical interventions to reduce suffering on a less grand scale.

In the years that have passed since Popper wrote *The Open Society and its Enemies*, we have learned a great deal about what works and what does not work in alleviating poverty. Universal free education, public housing, unemployment benefits, pensions for the elderly and disabled, and, in every affluent nation except the United States, universal health insurance, have done more to reduce human suffering than even the most benign attempts to introduce communism. There is still more to be learned, and much more to be done. At the time of writing, some governments and non-governmental organizations are experimenting, very much in the spirit of Popper's piecemeal social engineering, with the provision of a universal basic income that gives everyone, whether they work or not, sufficient income to live on. Some believe that we will need to introduce such an arrangement when robots and artificial intelligence make human workers redundant across a wide range of industries and professions. When that transformation comes, Marx's ideas about the role that economic interests play in our intellectual and political lives will remain relevant; his prediction of the inevitability of a proletarian revolution will not.

Note on sources

Chapter 2: The young Hegelian

The quotation from Engels is from 'Ludwig Feuerbach and the End of Classical German Philosophy', in K. Marx and F. Engels, *Selected Works* (Moscow: Foreign Languages Publishing House, 1951), vol. 2, pp. 364–6.

The quotation from Hegel is from *The Philosophy of History*, trans. J. Sibree, ed. C. J. Friedrich (New York: Dover, 1956), p. 19.

Chapter 3: From God to money

The quotation from Engels is from 'Ludwig Feuerbach and the End of Classical German Philosophy', in K. Marx and F. Engels, *Selected Works* (Moscow: Foreign Languages Publishing House, 1951), vol. 2, pp. 367–8.

The description of Moses Hess reaching communism by 'the philosophic path' is from F. Engels, 'Progress of Social Reform on the Continent', in *The New Moral World*, a small English journal, quoted in Robert Tucker's *Philosophy and Myth in Karl Marx* (Cambridge: Cambridge University Press, 1961), p. 107.

Chapter 5: The first Marxism

Engels described the materialist conception of history as Marx's chief discovery in his 'Speech at the Graveside of Karl Marx', in K. Marx and F. Engels, *Selected Works*, vol. 2, pp. 167–8.

Chapter 7: The goal of history

Engels describes Marx's denial that he is a Marxist in a letter to Starkenburg, 25 January 1894; Engels's letters to Schmidt (5 August 1890), to Bloch (21 September 1890), and to Mehring (14 April 1893) also deal with the interpretation of historical materialism. All are reprinted in L. S. Feuer (ed.), *Marx & Engels: Basic Writings on Politics and Philosophy* (New York: Doubleday Anchor, 1959).

Chapter 8: Economics

Engels described surplus value as the second of Marx's great discoveries in his 'Speech at the Graveside of Karl Marx', in K. Marx and F. Engels, *Selected Works*, vol. 2, pp. 167–8.

Paul Samuelson describes Marx as minor post-Ricardian in 'Wages and Interest: A Modern Dissection of Marxian Economic Models', *American Economic Review*, vol. 47 (1957), p. 911.

Chapter 9: Communism and revolution

Engels described Marx as a revolutionist in his 'Speech at the Graveside of Karl Marx', in K. Marx and F. Engels, *Selected Works*, vol. 2, pp. 167–8.

Evidence of Marx's openness to the possibility of a democratic transition comes from Karl Marx, 'On the Hague Congress: A Correspondent's Report of a Speech Made at a Meeting in Amsterdam on September 8 1872', Karl Marx and Friedrich Engels, *Collected Works*, vol. 23 (New York: International Publishers, 1975), p. 255; I owe this reference to Gareth Stedman Jones, *Karl Marx: Greatness and Illusion* (Cambridge, Mass.: Harvard University Press, 2016), p. 551. Engels's account of Marx's belief in the possibility of a peaceful and legal revolution in England is in his Preface to the 1886 English edition of *Capital*.

Engels's reference to 'a really human morality' occurs in his *Anti-Dühring*, also reprinted in Feuer (ed.), *Marx & Engels: Basic Writings on Politics and Philosophy* at p. 272.

Chapter 10: Was Marx right?

Hegel's comment about our desire for greater comfort comes from his *Philosophy of Right,* trans. T. M. Knox (London: Oxford University Press, 1967), paragraph 191, Addition.

On the likely evolutionary basis of a drive to reach the top, see Peter Singer, *A Darwinian Left: Politics, Evolution, and Cooperation* (New Haven: Yale University Press, 2000).

Chapter 11: Is Marx still relevant?

For the success of Deng's economic reforms in reducing poverty, see the World Bank's overview of China, <http://www.worldbank.org/en/country/china/overview>. On China's distribution of income, see the *CIA World Factbook*, <http://www.cia.gov/library/publications/the-world-factbook/rankorder/2172rank.html>. The quote from President Xi Jinping is from *China Reform Monitor*, No. 1233, 10 August 2016, <http://www.afpc.org/publication_listings/viewBulletin/3258>. The quote from Wang Weiguang is from *Social Sciences in China*, vol. 32, no. 4 (November 2011), p. 16.

Thomas Piketty's *Capital in the Twenty-First Century* was first published in French in 2013, and in English, trans. Arthur Goldhammer, by Harvard University Press in 2014.

For a neo-Marxist critique of Piketty, see John Bellamy Foster and Michael D. Yates, 'Piketty and the Crisis of Neoclassical Economics', *Monthly Review* (November 2014), pp. 1–24.

Marx's comments on free trade are in 'From our German Correspondent, the Free Trade Congress in Brussels', September 1847, and Karl Marx, 'Speech on the Question of Free Trade', 9 January 1848, both published in Karl Marx and Friedrich Engels, *Collected Works*, vol. 6 (New York: International Publishers, 1975), p. 290 and p. 465, respectively. I owe these references to Gareth Stedman Jones, *Karl Marx: Greatness and Illusion*, p. 233.

For Oxfam's campaign against inequality, see <http://www.oxfam.org/en/pressroom/pressreleases/2017-01-16/just-8-men-own-same-wealth-half-world>.

The World Bank's poverty estimates are at <http://www.worldbank.org/en/topic/poverty/overview>. For further discussion see

Peter Singer, *One World Now* (New Haven: Yale University Press 2016), pp. 95–104.

For a brief account of ecosocialism, see Michael Löwy, 'What is Ecosocialism?', *Capitalism Nature Socialism*, vol. 19 (2008), pp. 15–24.

For Karl Popper on utopian and piecemeal social engineering, see *The Open Society and Its Enemies*, vol. 1 (London: Routledge, 1945), pp. 138–48.

Marx

Further reading

Writings by Marx

Marx wrote so much that the definitive edition of all the writings of Marx and Engels (*Marx–Engels Werke*), published in East Germany from 1956 to 1990, consists of forty-five volumes. An English edition of the *Collected Works*, published by Lawrence and Wishart, was completed in 2005 and contains fifty volumes. As the list of abbreviations in the front matter suggests, I regard *Karl Marx: Selected Writings*, 2nd edition, edited by David McLellan (Oxford: Oxford University Press, 2000), as the best single-volume collection. *The Marx–Engels Reader*, 2nd edition, edited by Robert C. Tucker (New York: Norton, 1978), and *Karl Marx: Selected Writings*, edited by Lawrence H. Simon (Indianapolis: Hackett, 1994), are also widely used. Many of Marx's most important texts are in the public domain, at least in their older translations, and can be found online. The Marx Engels archive, at <http://www.marxists.org/archive/marx>, has a wide range of Marx and Engels's writings.

There are many editions of Marx's most famous works. The *Communist Manifesto* is a good place to begin reading Marx. It is available online. (Ironically Amazon, the global retail giant of the capitalist digital economy, offers it free in a Kindle edition.) There is also a Penguin edition, with an introduction by Gareth Stedman Jones (London, 2002). After reading the *Manifesto* and some selections from other texts, you may like to try the first volume of *Capital*. It is not as difficult as you might imagine, and is again available in a number of different editions. The Ben Fowkes translation

published by Penguin is now widely used, as is an earlier
translation originally published in the Soviet Union and freely
available online.

Writings about Marx

If the writings by Marx and Engels number fifty volumes, those about
Marx must run into the tens of thousands. Below is a *very* brief
selection of some better recent books. Although older works are
interesting because they enable us to see how earlier generations
conceived Marx, their ignorance of his unpublished early writings
and of the *Grundrisse* make them an unreliable guide to the
origins and basis of Marx's views.

There are several excellent accounts of Marx's life. Two acclaimed
biographies place Marx in his historical context: Gareth Stedman
Jones, *Karl Marx: Greatness and Illusion* (Cambridge, Mass.:
Harvard University Press, 2016), and Jonathan Sperber, *Karl
Marx: A Nineteenth-Century Life* (New York: Norton, 2013). For
many years the standard biography has been David McLellan's
Marx: A Biography, now in its fourth edition (New York: Palgrave
Macmillan, 2006). Francis Wheen's *Karl Marx: A Life* (New York:
Norton, 1999) is more popular in style.

An acquaintance with Hegel's ideas deepens one's understanding
of Marx, and if you have enjoyed this book, you may also like Peter
Singer, *Hegel: A Very Short Introduction* (Oxford: Oxford University
Press, 2001). The continuity between Marx's youthful Hegelian
writings and his mature work was first clearly demonstrated by
Robert Tucker, in *Philosophy and Myth in Karl Marx*, first
published in 1961, and now in its third edition (London: Routledge,
2000). David McLellan's *The Young Hegelians and Karl Marx*
(London: Macmillan, 1969) gives useful background to Marx's
intellectual development, as does *The Young Karl Marx: German
Philosophy, Modern Politics, and Human Flourishing*, by David
Leopold (Cambridge: Cambridge University Press, 2009). Bertell
Ollman, *Alienation: Marx's Conception of Man in Capitalist Society*
(2nd edn, Cambridge: Cambridge University Press, 1977), is more
readable than most works on alienation.

To balance the Hegelian emphasis of these works, G. A. Cohen's *Karl
Marx's Theory of History* (expanded edition, Princeton: Princeton
University Press, 2000) argues for a more old-fashioned

interpretation of Marxism as a scientific theory of history, an interpretation often known—disparagingly—as 'technological determinism'. Melvin Rader's *Marx's Interpretation of History* (Oxford: Oxford University Press, 1979) presents a wider range of possible interpretations. Cohen's later work, *If You're An Egalitarian, How Come You're So Rich?* (Cambridge, Mass.: Harvard University Press, 2000), discusses some broader ethical issues from a position sympathetic to Marx.

David Harvey's two-volume *A Companion to Marx's Capital* (London: Verso, 2010 and 2013) offers an introduction to Marx's major work. Harvey has also produced helpful video lectures corresponding to each chapter that are available on his website (<http://davidharvey.org/reading-capital/>). In *Marx, Capital and the Madness of Economic Reason* (Oxford: Oxford University Press, 2017), Harvey argues that *Capital* remains relevant today.

For a brief account of Marxist views on the environmental crisis, see Fred Magdoff and John Bellamy Foster, *What Every Environmentalist Needs to Know about Capitalism* (New York: Monthly Review Press, 2011); for a more extensive discussion, go to Fred Magdoff and Chris Williams, *Creating an Ecological Society: Toward a Revolutionary Transformation* (New York: Monthly Review Press, 2017). The topic is frequently discussed in the journal *Capitalism Nature Socialism*.

Étienne Balibar's *The Philosophy of Marx* (London: Verso, 2014) is a short but dense study of Marx and later Marxists from the perspective of continental European philosophy. Leszek Kolakowski presents the entire sweep of Marxist theory, from the founders through its 'Golden Age' to its dissolution into Soviet ideology, in *Main Currents of Marxism*, originally published in three volumes, but now available in one (New York: Norton, 2008).

Index

Marx

SOCIAL MEDIA
Very Short Introduction

Join our community
www.oup.com/vsi

- Join us online at the official Very Short Introductions **Facebook** page.
- Access the thoughts and musings of our authors with our online **blog**.
- Sign up for our monthly **e-newsletter** to receive information on all new titles publishing that month.
- Browse the full range of Very Short Introductions online.
- Read **extracts** from the Introductions for free.
- Visit our library of **Reading Guides**. These guides, written by our expert authors will help you to question again, why you think what you think.
- If you are a teacher or lecturer you can order inspection copies quickly and simply via our website.

ONLINE CATALOGUE
A Very Short Introduction

Our online catalogue is designed to make it easy to find your ideal Very Short Introduction. View the entire collection by subject area, watch author videos, read sample chapters, and download reading guides.

http://fds.oup.com/www.oup.co.uk/general/vsi/index.html